Norman Antonio Zelaya characters soar to life in Gente, Folks, prose stories that create a vibrant chorus of voices that illuminate San Francisco's Mission District, a neighborhood rich in history, culture, violence and loss, love and solidarity. Zelaya shows us a world where everyday survival is foremost, where family and community come not only from the heart, but from the soul. A wonderful new book by a talented writer.

Gail Tsukiyama, author of The Samurai's Garden and The Color of Air.

Zelaya's stories are testimonials to the spirit of San Francisco's Mission District, against the grinding forces of gentrification. In Zelaya's poetry-like prose, brief encounters on Muni, in the laundromat, or on the playground take on mystical significance. Reading Gente, Folks is like walking through time, simultaneously visiting with the ghosts of the Mission past, present, and-with hope-future.
May-lee Chai, author of Useful Phrases for Immigrants: Stories and Dragon Chica.

Zelaya is writing about the people in the Mission even God stopped thinking about. The youth, youngsters, and Gente, "stooped, moving quick, mechanical. Hardly seen," are magnified in these stories like sheet music leaping off the page, becoming audible in your ear. You wanna get up and hear the señoras and the doñas captured pitch perfectly. Zelaya is writing about a Mission District in danger of disappearing. Imagine a barrio whose football field is 15 yards too short and doesn't even have an endzone. Imagine this gente still building community around that field, still hungry to play, and to score. The heartbeat of La Mision is in this collection, to be sure, asking you to slow your roll, get on your knees, put your head on the sidewalk, and listen.

Joseph Rios, author of Shadowboxing: Poems and Impersonations (Omnidawn, winner 2018 American Book Award)

TO
CHRISTY + TONY
A SLICE OF
FRISCO LIFE!

—JOANNE
+
KEN

Gente,
Folks

Norman Antonio Zeleya

BFP
BLACK FREIGHTER PRESS

First Edition, 1st Printing

ISBN 13: 978-1-955953-00-9

Cover Art & Design: Adrian Garcia Gomez

Black Freighter Press
San Francisco, California

https://www.blackfreighterpress.com/

1.

Doña Lucero let it be known early on, first time we met, that she was tough on Osvaldo, *así soy siempre*. When she had to, she raised her voice with him, she was mano dura because she wanted him to be raised with educación, she all alone was bringing up Osvaldo because that's the way things had turned out, *desgraciadamente*, the boy's father was a good-for-nothing and only came around when his vices permitted him, when he wasn't too busy with his women o su licor, *el cabrón que es, bastard, perdóname, Maestro, pero yo hablo así*, that had always been her manner of speaking, *francamente, con la verdad*, she said, with the truth *sin pelos en la lengua* and I bowed my head knowingly, of course, señora, and I urged her to continue with an open hand *por favor…*

…*Bueno, Maestro*, the father only comes around to mess up the boy and spoil him with candy and toys and video games on his phone, *lo peor*, the worst he can do because Osvaldo becomes obsessed, you should see him, his eyes bug out, Maestro, and then I have to correct Osvaldo when he doesn't want to give back his father's phone, or worse, he starts to tantrum for my telephone, *y pide y pide y pide*, and his father doesn't help, he berates me *hija de la fregada, dirty slut, no sirves para nada, you're useless* and he yells at me to give the boy what he wants, *déjalo*, he says, *dáselo*, he says, *hija de su puta madre*, he says *y de ahí no me baja* that's where he's always had me, low, a worthless tramp, because that's all he knows to say to me *soy puta, a whore*, and he says it with no shame, doesn't matter that Osvaldo is there between us *en frente de mijo, Maestro, y Osvaldo shrieking, llorando pero llantos*, face streaked, mouth dribbling until he throws himself to the floor kicking and thrashing and his father all the time yelling at me, cursing me, vulgarities, nastiness *que solamente sirves para chingar, y que tu chingada madre, y que puta y no sé que y no sé cuanto*, and Osvaldo screeching harder each time, *pataleando*, and the whole world staring at me. Confused, stunned. *Qué vergüenza*. I want to hide but where, *dime donde*. No, no no, I put up with enough of that life, that's why I left him *mejor que él chinga a su madre, perdón Maestro, it's rude, vulgar that I speak that way pero yo voy a sacar a mijo adelante*, I'm going to raise Osvaldo to respect my word and obey me, obey others, too, and do what's right, Osvaldo is going to know that he's coming to school to learn and that here he's going to listen to the teacher and he's going to do his work *sin berrinche*, not one blowup, and there isn't going to be no Walgreens ni Cheetos ni *Sponge Bob* ni Takis ni *Star Wars* cars ni Espiderman stickers... *mira Maestro, se lo juro* each time we pass by la Walgreens, it's another toy, any little thing, and each one is $4 – $5, *imagínase Maestro*, the cost *y yo sin dinero*, and the house is so full of these little thingies I don't know where to put them anymore, but if I don't buy him something, then it's a complete spectacle *berrinche, Maestro*, flipped over in the middle of la Walgreens like a sick crab, no no no, I can't go on like that, *Maestro, por eso le hablo fuerte*, when I have to raise my voice at him, I do, *fuerte*, because I want Osvaldo to learn, *he can learn*, and I want him to know he has to respect everyone. That's what I want, Maestro.

I listened and promised her that Osvaldo was going to learn in my classroom. She was right. All children could learn. That was my work. Every day. For everyone. As long as students were in my class. Anyone who came through that door.

And a time later, Doña Lucero hadn't changed neither her manner nor her goal as she led Osvaldo by the hand through the neighborhood on a chilly December morning. He was two years older, and paunchier, head shaven clean and perfectly round. I saw them pass the mural of Santana on 19th and Mission, thrown up on the side of what used to be an Army recruitment office. Once upon a time. It was a check cashing/envio place now. Only folks that knew knew. As little kids, we had no idea what their aim was on that corner, we just knew they gave cool T-shirt iron-ons for free. Fierce eagle heads. Tanks. Gold stars and stripes. Thick and tacky across our chests as we ran around playing keep-away on a concrete baseball field, scattered and frantic. Nothing military about us.

Doña Lucero looked military though — her dark hair swept up into a tidy bun, elbow tucked over her purse. Osvaldo shuffled quick-like on the balls of his feet to keep up, flapping his free hand. La doña wasn't worried if he fell. Not a thought that he might stumble. Her eyes were forward, resolute in her expression. They had somewhere to go, man, and she was getting them there. The word was pertinacious.

I watched them walk away. I thought about them, about Doña Lucero mostly. *Esa señora es firme* was what my Chicano brothers and sisters would've said to me about her. I wasn't quite sure what it meant to be *firme,* but I had an idea. It was this woman determined to bring her child through this world, this unkind bureaucracy of take-a-number and have-a-seat, of cheap carpeting, flickering lights and bullet-proof glass, take him by the wrist and follow blue arrows through narrow corridors only to sit and wait, sit and wait in another dull room until her number hit. It was filling out reams of applications, stopping many times to get up and stick her head in the mouth hole of a window to ask for help, apologizing, *la molestia, su ignorancia,* she didn't understand, her thick finger on a line, what did this mean, if she didn't have that, did that hurt her son, was there nothing for him if she didn't have that document, no, no, it was fine, she just had to fill out the rest as best she could. Then it was sit and wait, sit and wait for an interview, and a thank you for her time, she'd receive a letter of approval for services and next steps, or a letter declining her request. It was a tenacious Doña Lucero, impatient and afraid they might tell her no, she went back to the offices to ask if Osvaldo had been approved yet, she hadn't gotten her letter but she knew Osvaldo'd be approved, pestered until she was sent to follow arrows down corridors, where she stuck her head in several glass mouth holes until they granted Osvaldo services. It was a solemn Doña Lucero with a thick clutch of papers gathered in a manila folder to present to teachers, proof, *aquí está, maestros,* whatever they needed to teach Osvaldo, whatever they needed, they only had to ask, please, *por favor, maestros, aquí está,* a small fat hand slapped the folder, whatever else *díganme,* please, please, she held the sheath formally in her level palms, smiled as kind as she could. Anything she could do, they only had to ask.

    That's what it meant to be *firme.* Doña Lucero was *firme* as fuck, *chinga su madre.* That was love. For real. Sometimes it was masked by a briskness, an impatience with wanting to be heard, *perdóname Maestro*, for cutting you off; or by the despair of asking why, why is my son this way. It was overcome by the shame of having to respond to *gente* who wondered out loud what's wrong with your *hijo*, or worse yet, by her guilt, self-blame like what did I do, was it my fault, Maestro, did I do this somehow *sin querer*. It looked curt, ungracious at times, but it was love for real, unconditional, *amor de madre*. Damn it.

I remembered Osvaldo's emphatic refusal to go to school, I heard them coming down the hallway, the *no quiero escuela* getting progressively louder until they appeared in the doorway, my students calling out, *buenos días, Osvaldo*, unfazed, busy connecting cubes in groups of five or ten. It was *no quiero, no quiero, NO QUIERO*, each and every single day as Doña Lucero dropped him off, late, 30 minutes into the school day, in spite of her best efforts, *lo juro maestro*, they left early *pero mira*, Osvaldo big and red stamping his feet as she gave him instructions to *pórtate bien, escucha al maestro*, and then she entered into brief negotiations as he clutched her waist, *Osvaldo, quieres Loud House cartoons – sí, mamá. Quieres Loud House – sí, mamá. Ok, entonces* listen to Maestro and at home *te doy el Loud House*. But as she moved to leave, Osvaldo screamed and grabbed his mother's wrist, *no no, wait, un beso, un beso, mamá – ok, un beso y me voy*, so she kissed the top of his head but then he threw his arms around her neck and held on for dear life, *ya Osvaldo, ya – un beso, mamá, te quiero decir algo… Osvaldo, Osvaldo…* And at that point I had to intervene, slipped between them so Doña Lucero could pry herself loose and walk away, Osvaldo collapsed over my shoulder, sobbing miserably, slobber soaking into my shirt. Doña Lucero steamed down the middle of the wide hallway, fists pumping low at her sides, her mind rolling through all the things she needed to get done before she made her way back to pick up Osvaldo at the end of the day.

Eventually, three weeks or so, Osvaldo learned the classroom routine and was happy and curious and liked to listen to stories. He sat with me and one other student and we did picture walks of storybooks before I directed them to read, but his first move was always *no quiero leer*.

Osvaldo?

No quiero.

Osvaldo, how do you get what you want?

No quiero leer. NO!

Doña Lucero had told me to call her if I ever struggled with Osvaldo, so then I'd move for the phone.

No! Sorry, Maestro, sorry, Maestro.

How do you get what you want?

Palabras amables. Kind words.

Gracias, Osvaldo.

No call mamá?

Let's read, Osvaldo.

I'm sorry. Un beso, Maestro —

No, Osvaldo, let's read.

Un beso mamá?

Sí, Osvaldo, a kiss for your mother.

You sad, Maestro?

No, Osvaldo. Let's read.

OK, Maestro… And he'd point to a word and furrow his brow.

That was all you, señora. Osvaldo learned just like you said he would.

Osvaldo sifted through the packets of game cards, named the characters illustrated on the metallic wrappers, described softly to himself what each did, their powers, strengths, what they did in the cartoons. He set them on a shelf among rubber squeak toys as he pulled packets one by one.

Osvaldo, ya nos vamos.

This one, mama. It's Charmander.

Hoy no, mijo. Vámonos.

Doña Lucero explained that he already had many cards at home and the little figurines, and they needed to hurry because she had to leave dinner ready, she was working late, and she was going to leave him his favorite, chicken breasts *milanesas*, so they needed to hurry. *Nos apuramos* and she would give him a pudding cup and he could play a game on her phone when they got home.

Osvaldo held the thin packet in both hands, studied it. *Vámonos, mijo.* He grunted, stamped both feet. They were in a hurry, she repeated. Doña Lucero took the packet from him, tossed it aside and took his wrist. He pulled away and stood defiant in the aisle. *Osvaldo, por favor – Charmander, mama, OK? Just one this time.* She waved at him to take her hand. *Charmander.* She said no, and he lost it. He dropped to his bottom and threw himself backward, writhing and pounding his fists. Doña Lucero stood firm and repeated her direction, *vámonos por favor*, her hand out. Osvaldo got to his feet and began to run circles in the aisle. He managed two whirls in the cramped space before he slammed sharply into the shelves. He staggered back, stunned, touched his mouth. He saw blood on his fingers. Both his upper and lower lips ripped against his teeth, filling his mouth with blood. Osvaldo picked at his gums then he saw more blood, redder, on his hand and screamed. He wailed, dreadful. Doña Lucero approached with open hands to calm him. She reached for his face. Suddenly, Osvaldo ran out of the aisle, past his mother, past the people in line, past the cashiers, and out of the store.

Osvaldo!

She swiped at and missed him as he stormed away. Customers in line watched, unmoved, as the exasperated mother run after her child.

Osvaldo stopped at the corner, toes over the curb and holding his lip. He looked down into the gutter, let a thread of bloody spit drip onto the grate. Larger globs plopped cherry red and he whimpered. He stepped off the curb, mouth covered, and walked, no mind to direction or place or the people he bumped against. They turned him every which way, frustrated him, bothered him, and he whimpered louder, eyes watery and hands covered in rosy saliva. The crowd moved in currents and Osvaldo was lost.

Doña Lucero made it outside and scanned the streets.

She saw him in the crosswalk, scared, stricken as people moved around him. She stepped off the corner, but Osvaldo spotted her, remembered how angry he was and ran. Doña Lucero saw it coming. The black SUV was enormous, monstrously boxy alongside surging pedestrians. In a back seat, a woman cared for her baby. The seatbelt was across the young mother's chest, the baby safely strapped in a carrier. She looked fondly into the little face, adjusted the blanket around the chubby cheeks. She was in her world with her baby, talking nonsense, cooing, as she touched the button nose. The joy filled her eyes. Her precious bundle. That was all she saw.

2.

There's a small pond in the pit on 22nd Street and Mission. After a 4 alarm fire burned down the large apartment building, dozens of units charred and exposed like dung beetles turned over legs to the sky, months later bulldozers came and knocked down the hollowed blackened shell left behind, and then cleaned out the foundation. It wasn't only apartments. It was dental offices, from teeth cleanings to braces; and a travel agency that promoted Taca Airlines and covered the walls with posters of Pan Am offering future flights to the moon; tax preparers and immigration lawyers, who were all notary publics that could officiate weddings, too. An entire ground floor of commercial spaces, the Mission Market with produce and meat, beef, pork, chicken de rancho, fresh chorizo and longaniza strung across the back wall; a florist tucked in a space no bigger than a toll booth, where she stood all day clipping stems and curling pink and red listones with her shears; a Cambodian doughnut shop, enormous glazed braids, heavy apple fritters, the ladies chattering all at once to serve *what else, what else, you want coffee*; a barber sitting in his single chair with the newspaper snapped open, waiting for walk-ins; La Alteña taqueria with a deep salsa bar and specialty fish tacos, Ensenada-style; a shoe store that also sold ladies fashions; a tailor, a young girl who had worked years for the old man who had his tailor shop for decades just up the street, but he didn't listen, never got the hems right because he was a square and his tastes hadn't changed since he arrived in the barrio in 1975, and he wasn't nearly as hip as '75, but she was cool, had a touch; a pupusa stand, the two doñas forever backs to the customers, fleshy arms working, their sixth sense on, *qué quieres, amor*; and Popeye's Chicken, a line out the door every Tuesday. At one time, that was a video arcade, where I got hip to Super Pac-Man and Donkey Kong Jr, the new shit. The building was five stories of bustling life. How did the people on the upper floors get out through those narrow hallways, soles and heels sticking to the nylon runners that covered them? No one took the elevators. Antique cages only moved four passengers at a time. No one dropped the ladders from the fire escapes. They stepped quickly as they could, hands on the shoulders of those in front, descended the squared staircases that spiraled down the center of the building, deafening with shouts and clanging of alarms and stifling and smoky. But they all made it out. Except for one viejito. *El pobre.* The fire raged for hours. It lit up the sky, amber gleam surging against the blackness. Typically, the sky was starless because of the streetlamps and neon signs along Mission. It was dull, forgettable. But that night, the sky was immense, fathomless. It moved, gaping. There had to be lots of smoke, billowing. It was lost in all that pitch.

The emptiness left behind is enormous. Deep and rectangular like a landfill. The pit reminds me of the one left behind on 16th and Valencia, where a hotel burned, The Gartland, condemned and later destroyed by landlord arson when I was a kid. Twelve dead. That cavity lasted years. Chain link fencing and plywood sheets tried to keep people out but there were gaps where the fence was held together loosely, and after a while it said *fuck it* and fell apart. It was a reluctant cemetery. 7 women, 4 men, and a little kid, 21 months. There was sadness, anger. People built altars and trash sculptures in there and painted graffiti murals on the walls, letters ten foot high that stretched several yards across. 12 DEAD/ LANDLORD ARSON! In the winter, the pit filled with pools of gray murky water, a cream muck floating, swirling. I stood on the street in the rain looking way down to the floor, fingers curled on the wire, as puddles formed and the dirt darkened. Sometimes there were candles on the altars, the ones in the tall glass jars that they sold at the Walgreens. They were lit and I saw them flicker in the dim afternoon light. I waited to see if the raindrops would put the candles out. How did the people crawl down there, it must have been like jumping into an empty pool, tiled walls slick and the lip unreachable, so then how did they get out, I thought.

For weeks, it's rained like when I was little, and now there is a pond on 22nd Street. The bulldozers are gone and the bottom is covered with wild grass and weeds like dandelion and sour grass and anise and foxtails and city wheat. Thick and overgrown, proudly natural. Someone climbed over the black wrought iron fence to plant a bright pink rosebush. It's almost beautiful. There are frogs in there now. I hear them at night when I walk home from doing laundry. I stop and peek through the sturdy bars. The water is unbroken, a few lights reflect off its surface, but I can't see anything move. Then suddenly, the misplaced racket echoes. The croaking is pleasant. It sounds like joy. But how did they get in there? They can't be red-legged frogs. Those are the only frogs native to San Francisco, but they're rare, endangered. They're found in few places in the city, spots in Golden Gate Park, maybe Glen Park Canyon, but they couldn't have made it here alone. They're little frogs. Maybe someone let a pet bullfrog loose, or somehow frog eggs made it to the water carried by a bird. I don't know but there are definitely frogs croaking in the pit.

They're loud at night, and you can hear them if you stop and stand still.

3.

I'm filling my tank at the Olympic, the cheap gas on South Van Ness. A few others are filling up, too. It's a lazy time of day, in between traffic peaks. A man ambles near the station, checks the door of the green public restroom booth. He puts a hand on a meter; it used to take coins. Damn progress. He's middle aged, maybe early 50s, a white man, lean from being on the street. His forearms are muscular, shiny with sweat, smudged with grease. His hair is longish and thick with oil. He shuffles among the cars.

A dude in an old Impala wagon calls out to him.

Hey, do you collect cans?

Excuse me?

Do you collect cans?

He scratches his crown, Do I have to?

Here man, I have some cans you can sell.

The haggard man, face grooved and ruminating, walks over to the open trunk and the dude hands him a plastic garbage bag, full and brassy. He takes the bag and walks off down to Chavez. He stops at the corner and surveys the traffic, cars rushing west to St. Luke's Hospital and Twin Peaks and the Pacific, trucks and vans speeding east to the freeway and Evans Street and the Produce District. The light changes for left or right turns, depending on whether one needs to make the bridge, awful with gridlock, exhaust in the eyes, or one's having a cheat day, playing hooky and dreaming of the ocean, the Pacific a forever dream come true. The old man puts the bag down like he's spent, drained. He squints in the daylight, scratches his cheek. He looks up and down the thoroughfare. The light changes. He doesn't move. It's mid-morning, bright.

It's a hot day. It's a fucking hot ass day.

4.

Juriel comes down the sidewalk. Khaki Ben's and white Niners jersey, the red 16 pulled over his swollen belly. His steps are choppy but quiet. He's out over his toes. Like a toddler. He's exposed, his red jacket rumpled and open. There's a shine to his unshaven face. He looks at the pavement as he goes, an uncertain stare, his face something worrisome, *preocupado*. Then he sees me and he lights up.

    Tío, me regalas un dólar, tío?

    He says it like I would say it, *un dólar*. He grew up here like I did. He's from these streets like I am. He's familiar to me like other heads I crossed in the neighborhood. He's a ghost of barrio past. I can picture him. He wasn't a dude that got into games. First, it was resting against the fence as homeboys ran full courts. He just watched, talked mild shit, *that was your eye, Guillermo, ha, caballo*. Then he guarded the boom box as old heads played softball, *hey batter, batter*, checked the EQ and tossed fouls back to the infield, careful not to drop his cigarette. And finally, he posted up on the block, cracked his beer sloppy, talking 'bout *remember, hey, remember... but no wait, check it out, broder, right, it was like this, check it out, maje, I'm talking, we was kicking back, right...* slurp and *asco* face, *naw, blood, let me tell it.* Juriel's version was hyperbole *she was hella fine, right, she had big gato eyes, and I was charming her, had her laughing at my little jokes and shit, talking to her all close*, slurp and *asco* face, he mimed and made big faces as he recounted how this fine ass girl was into him, things getting better by the minute, *you feel me*, a cough and beer dribbled on his chin, then dudes burst his bubble, talking 'bout, man, she was laughing at him, chocolate all on his face and shirt and shit, *no jodas, that ain't true, blood*, his homeboys broke up, drowned out his story, talked over him until Juriel gave up telling the tale, and cracked another beer as he checked the EQ, grinned, *forget you guys*, a funny shuffle, slurp and *asco* face. *You guys don't know. Shiiit.* He closed his eyes, heard the music. Forget you. He wasn't going to waste his time. Better he just listened to his jam.

He's from these streets like I am. He's younger than me though. Ten years, a little less. 'He didn't make it' is something I might say to someone who knows what I'm talking about. *Remember him.* Saw him the other day. Yeah, not good.

Juriel stops and receives me with arms slightly open. *Just a dollar, tío.* His eyes are glassy, syrupy. He quakes faintly as he holds it together. Hopeful. All he has to do is be patient. Offer a half smile. *Un dólar*, like I say it.

I shake my head, a prescribed no. But I look at him when I say it. Sorry, bro.

Juriel changes. Resigned. He takes a drag off his cigarette and drops back into his disillusion. He checks his jacket pocket, both sides, feels for a lighter, maybe a key. Then he walks on, strangely, hovering over the sidewalk.

I don't act like it, but there's a sadness in me about him. Something like grief. I can't give him anything this time, like I might other times. I do have a little money on me. I just can't give it. I need to keep it. All. But he knows what I'm talking about.

5.

It's a short ride from Fruitvale to San Francisco. The trip through the tube is loud, roaring. But it's over quick. Three other people are in the car. One scrolls on her phone. The second reads a thick paperback. The third just stares ahead, rocks with the train. He cradles a basketball to his hip, his other hand peaceful on his knee. Then he comes awake like an animatronic robot, the body stirring in sections until he's picking his hair out in stiff, combative motions. He rocks, stims, on the edge of the seat. He has a stick of lip balm in his hand and runs it all over his forehead and cheeks. He tucks it in his shirt pocket, stims more. No one pays him any mind.

His voice is forceful, articulate. He's like talk radio:

Brothers are running out of clothes. Now I'm getting back to the Bruce Lee thing. I can only watch. I'm only half black. I can only watch. There goes that feeling. I got the secret in my pocket. I pray in quarter steps. The god we're thinking of is the god that's killing us. I know. I can only watch.

Do you know how old Bruce Lee is now? That's what I'm saying. That's a lifetime between you and him. Between us and the new style. An open hand, it can break you down in your chest, forceful, move you back several feet and nothing you can do about it. Or it can offer help. That's what I'm saying. You getting saved by a 200-hundred-year-old-man.

I used to steal. Those days are over. Because I don't drink. Now I can only watch.

He runs more lip balm across his forehead, several passes,

rubs it into his skin. The train stops and he checks the station. Not his stop so he relaxes back into the seat. But it occurs to him to double check. So, he curls his head around the door then quickly grabs the basketball off the seat, and he slips into the crowd swarming on the platform. He checks his afro, applies more balm, and wades against them.

6.

Lissette is a young woman, a girl really, in a cream-colored dress, a sheath, too short. She leans against the corner, her crossed arms pressed firmly against her breast. A silver Lexus creeps and she breaks into a little trot. The car follows her, and the driver shouts profane and angry as he pulls alongside her, but Lissette keeps walking, screens her face with her dainty hand. *You gonna come around. You gonna have to.* A public works truck rolls up behind the Lexus and stays on its tail until the driver is forced to peel away. *Gonna have to.* Lissette heads back to the corner. She adjusts the small shawl draped around her shoulders. It covers her to the elbows but she tries to fit the rest of herself in. Her knees knock. She wonders whether dude will come back. It doesn't matter. Whatever. She stifles a shiver and waits, like the old woman does across from the school up the street, unwearyingly, curled in a folding chair on a corner, coat buttoned neck to ankles, next to her strawberry stand all afternoon, calling *fresas* to each passerby as she peels peanuts in her lap. Lissette waits like that. A block away, a motor revs, a garbage truck rumbles under the lights on 24th Street. Then it fades. Lissette thinks about going to a pumpkin patch when she was little. She didn't see any of the trip along the coast because she was too small to see out the window. It was all high green back of the bench seat and a pale blue sky, a few cottonlike clouds that must've left shadows on the water below. It was good that she couldn't see how high the school bus was above the ocean, how close it was to the edge of the cliff the whole time. She watched the sky dreamily until they arrived and the door opened to a patch that reached out to golden hills, and hundreds of pumpkins scattered everywhere. Sister Regina said the students could pick one pumpkin each. They streamed out into the rows, grabbing and lifting all manner of pumpkins, small and oblong and reddish and white and covered in warty bumps. Lissette walked patiently through the patch, stepped carefully in between pumpkins, squatted to look close, stroked the rind. She didn't pick any up. She crept along low to the ground, inspected as much with her hands as she did with her eyes until finally, she settled on a perfectly round, symmetrical pumpkin. It was large and she struggled to carry it. One of the chaperone mothers tried to convince her to take a small one, it was better for little children, but Lissette ignored her and huffed towards the bus, stopped to rest the pumpkin on the ground a couple times, but she carried it herself the whole way. On the drive home, she hugged the pumpkin, tight, so it didn't fall, and thought about how much fun it was to ferret around the patch and farm, all the colors, splotchy orange and green pumpkins, strawberries, black olallieberries, peaches, plums, mangoes, avocados.

Lissette pulls the shawl to better cover her elbows. She wishes she had a crate to sit on. It's 4:30 in the morning, and it's cold.

A white pick-up truck turns the corner slowly but doesn't stop for her. That's fine. She's busy minding the chill in her arms. Her feet tap the sidewalk. Likely he'll come around a second time for her. If he doesn't, someone else will. Lissette thinks about the dude in the Lexus but fuck him. Fuck that guy.

Above her, a light goes on in a window. The sheer curtain

glows green. No one moves inside. It's too early to get ready for school. But still time to get up.

7.

Joey spoke his first words when he was three. And when he did, it was rocks, inside the large planters that his mother kept in the house, in the living room, along a windowsill above the sink in the kitchen, on the landing at the top of the stairs, he found small stones that he lined along the inside of all the pots. Outside, he gathered rocks and stones and lined them on the edges of his mother's flower beds, sorted them by color and tone and created borders in repeating patterns. He spent hours probing the dark, damp earth under the lilac and camellia bushes, gently, inquisitive, brushed back the topsoil with little hands like spatulas, revealing worms and pill bugs and ground beetles and tiny slugs until he uncovered the rock he needed, it had to be the right size, the right color, the right shape, the right grain. He built simple but elegant geometric boundaries, told mama that he had greys and browns and creams and asked *mama, what comes next, mama, what comes next,* but didn't wait for his mother to respond *brown rock* he said as he laid out the stones carefully, precisely. Then one day he looked up and followed the length of oblong, elliptical, scalloped leaves from the leafstalk to the midrib to the very tip, brushed, poked, lightly pulled the point with pliant fingertips. The narrow, linear leaves were his favorites. He studied all the types, talked to himself as he passed leaves between his thumb and index finger, traced the margins, toothed, lobed, wavy, his soft narration unbroken, rhythmic, punctuated with tapping and reflection on a new detail, *like a heart, a heart-shape, like a heart.* It made his mother happy, buoyant to hear him talking. She never interrupted him. She read.

She wrote letters. She filled crossword puzzles while she listened to Joey like playing 45s. And then his mother introduced him to planting beans and the wonder of life, growth, care, every day slightly different, a leaf unfurled, the stem altered, tilted, more than the day before. The cheerfulness and ambition of the curling vines *look mama, they climb* and the excitement at the speed and agility *mama, it grabs*. Joey watered and cared for bean stalks in little milk cartons, terracotta pots, an abandoned aquarium, a work boot, one of his own sneakers. He cared for them from flower to bean. His mother had to give them away as they cluttered the yard and paths around the house, windowsills, the stairwell, the garage, the front steps, she gave them new homes so Joey could plant more, she promised they'd be taken care of as she handed the waxed cartons to his father, who dumped them in the park. Joey played with the soil, took pleasure in the graininess between his fingers. He loved planting. Until one day, he saw football.

Saturdays I bugged everybody to play tackle football at Mission High School. During the week, we played at the playground on the concrete field from the afternoon into the evening. It was all we had and it was cool, all the homeboys in the barrio came by to play, lots of times we had eleven on both sides and dudes subbed into the game as the day went and other dudes left, an errand, dinner, homework, smoke some weed, a TV show, pinball, somebody's sister showed up talking about let's go, a girlfriend came and crossed her arms, leaned against a fence with a cigarette, another homeboy with a joint, hungry, run to the store for chips and candy, Atari, comics, hopped on bikes and rode off, just got fucking bored. It was cool. But I wanted to play for real, I wanted to hit and tackle. I wanted to run that extra length of field, like I might keep on going. Count down by fives. Games at the playground was like running around in the living room, or playing one on one in the hallway with my little brother. Mama shouted to stop our sanganadas, *que hacen*. There were twelve of us in a one-bedroom apartment, and I was always looking for a place to play, a space to lay out my green army men, a shelf to stack my comics, a cigar box to hide my prized baseball cards and silver rings I found in the street. I forever shared a bed, shook legs off me and jousted with feet to claim space. I was always squirming to move a few inches further. I was always trying to pull out of arms. Break free. And I got fucking sick of ripping up my knees on the concrete, busting old scabs. Most neighborhood fools were satisfied with the playground, they didn't want to walk all the way to Mission High *aww fuck that*. But all I needed to do was convince Hugo. He was cool to me. He listened. *Alright, little man. Run ahead. Go deep*. And then he rallied all the other fucks. The Mission varsity team played all their league games at Kezar Stadium because the school field was only 85 yards long. It wasn't even long enough for two end zones. The JV played home games at Mission, but they had to walk the ball back 25 yards anytime anyone got inside the 20 yard line. It was always a regulation field for us though. It was dreams. Wishes. For real. Sometimes the big heads from the different gangs played each other at the field. San Fran Mission, 22nd Street Homeboys, Happy Holmes Grande, Little Time Mission, Tiny Winos. We stood on the sidelines, sipping on orange soda and working hard taffy, tossed a ball around and watched. At halftime, the big heads opened coolers of beer and dug into buckets of fried chicken and coleslaw. A girlfriend lit a joint and passed it around, gave her man a charge. Heads smoked weed throughout the game, actually. Music played and dudes bopped, digging it heavy. Halftime for real. The beer and food wasn't for us. Not for all of us. Harold, because he was older, and Hugo, whose brothers knew and ran with all them, got food. Hugo snuck us some drumsticks. Harold didn't. He was a prick talking 'bout *whatchu gonna give me though.* Dickhead. When the mood lulled, the big heads started shouting. They yelled at us to play the little heads from the other side. Not to be pussies and challenge them. *C'mon, fuckers, play.* We were hesitant to take the field. We felt their eyes, and worse, heard all their shit talking. It was pressure to be good. They cheered and laughed and goaded us to hurt each other. *C'mon, little man, you gonna let that chump do that to you? He ain't about shit! He's a bitch. Man, they talkin about your mama. Get that bitch. Pussies.* Chugging beers and spitting and talking all that shit. It got to us. The way to drown it out was to play hard. Get mean. Fight if we had to. When the big heads were ready to get their game going again, they crushed their empties, shouted *the fuck off the field, assholes,* and we shuffled to the sideline. We took a knee, checked our scrapes as we watched them play. Fools tried for a piece of chicken, hoped one of the homegirls would defend them if a big head barked to keep their hands out of the fucking cooler *don't be mean, it's just chicken, you dick.* We checked our pockets for gum, change, flicked rubber bands at each other until we got bored and decided to go because it got fucking boring to watch a bunch of high ass cholos in Chuck Taylors and tube socks scrum and yank at each other. After a while, we were like fuck it, and left for home.

But we loved tackle football, and whenever the field was free, and we got enough dudes together, we showed up super early to play.

One day after a night of heavy rain, the field was misty and damp. Large puddles flooded the corners. The sideline was marshy, spotted with clumps of crabgrass. It was a dreary scene. Behind the far sideline, laundry weighted down lines crisscrossing the backside of apartment buildings, a frugal web, the wooden stairs still dark, rows of sad tenement windows like glassy eyes. Everything was dripping. And the sky threatened. Hugo stepped onto the field and thudded his heel into the turf.

Is it muddy and shit?

No, it's good to play.

Hugo immediately started throwing passes to dudes to warm up.

Awright then. Let's pick teams.

We circled up, hands on our hips like the pros. Harold and Big Mario called team captains and split everybody up into two sides.

Check him out.

In the end zone near Church Street, this kid in a white Niners jersey was rolling on the ground, running plays by himself.

The broad sleeves flapped as he ran around. He looked to be about 16. He had mussed dirty blond hair and was strong looking. The number 49 was taut across his back. He hiked the ball, tossed it up between his legs and when the ball fell to the ground, he pounced on it, tackled himself. Sometimes he knocked the football loose and scrambled after it, recovered it, and came up cheering. He spiked the ball high into the air and circled the field in victory.

What the fuck is dude doing?

He's playing football, goofy ass. Hugo fired passes like a machine, his fingers curled on the follow through, all style. What's it look like?

The kid reset the ball and readied for a goal line stand, his fists dug into the turf. He scraped the ground with his feet like a bull. He called out a *red 14, red 14, set hut* then swung past the ball and flung himself at an imaginary quarterback. He tumbled and got quickly to his feet, a fierce roar and dance, index fingers to the sky and wiggling his ass awkward. Again, he ran around the field, arms raised. Winner.

Joey was dressed and standing by the kitchen door, turning his football anxiously in his hands. He rocked on the balls of his feet, ready. *Mama, I have to practice football. It rained all night, honey. It'll be all muddy and yucky. Mama, I have to practice.* Joey normally went out with his father in the afternoon to catch passes, to pass block, to run routes, he was clinical, *ok, dad, I'm going to go 5 yards out*, and he put a hand in the ground then sprinted 5 yards and broke to the sideline, hands out, thumbs together, then 10 yards, then 15 yards, *dad, I'm running down and in now*, his father began to complain about his shoulder after twenty minutes, an old high school injury, not a spring chicken, take it easy on your old man, son, *three more, dad, then we take a knee*, his father indulged Joey until he couldn't throw anymore and spent the rest of the time designing routes and watching his boy run. Clapped him up, cheered. Gave a big thumbs up. But that morning his father wasn't about to venture into the slop. He was too old to manage not slipping in the muck. *Listen to your mother, Joe. Not today. Mama, I have to practice. Your father said no, Joey.* And he stood in front of her, concern frozen in his brow, gripping his ball, fretful, ready, he was going to stay ready to play. His mother studied him, he had grown so much in the last year, he was taller than her, my god, he was more than nearly a man, she touched his curly bangs, swept them to the side, wished out loud that he would comb his hair more often. Joey gripped the football, massaged it as he waited, he stayed ready. His father had said it wasn't a good day to go out, the field had to be soaked after last night and it was forecast for even more rain, he was going to ruin his jersey. *Mama, it's football, I have to practice.* She touched his cheek. Sighed. *You make sure you do your best, honey. I'm going to be a 49er. Yes, darling, you are. You're a star, honey. My star.* She gave him a kiss on the cheek. He drew back, apprehensive, not being able to help himself, it made him feel something he couldn't explain, but Joey knew, he was going to be able to go. He shuffled his feet, revved up, *be safe, Joey* and hustled out of the house down a few blocks and across the street to the high school, drab and streaked and dismal.

We stood arms crossed, hands on hips, and stared. The kid played defense, practiced swim moves over and over, covered ground sideline to sideline until, finally, he scooped the ball up and ran the length of the field into the end zone and scored, punctuated by a somersault. He stood in victory V, howled at the leaden clouds. All alone. Touchdown.

He's really playing a game and shit.

Fuckin' trippin'. Dude's mental.

You guys talk too much shit. Hugo dropped seven steps and pump faked. Then he dropped three and double pumped. Let's kick off already.

But we ain't got even teams. We need one more.

Ask him to play.

Him?

What the fuck else we gonna do?

We shouted all at once, raucous and unclear. Then Javier stepped up.

Hey man! Dude!

He turned around, arms still raised.

Yeah man — you. Come play with us.

Javier waved him over. A few of us did.

The dude nodded his head hella enthusiastic. He picked up his football and jogged over. He was just a kid like us looking to play ball. But he was put together. He grew as he approached, his steps heavy. The football looked like a quail sheltered in his hands.

What's your name, man?

Joey.

Play with us, Joey. We need one more.

'Kay. Use my ball.

It was an official NFL football, smooth and leather, stitched, unlike the bloated rubber ball we had. Joey tossed it gently into the group. We threw it around, admired it, a for real NFL football, like the fuckin 49ers played with. Montana to Clark and shit. Fuckin live. Right on, Joey.

The teams jogged to opposite sides and kicked off. On the return, Harold caught the ball and headed straight up the middle of the field. Joey made a beeline to the ball, walked through everybody and flung himself at Harold's legs. He tried to high step out of his grasp, but Joey grew like long ass arms and wrapped up his ankles.

Holy shit! Fuckin dude came to play.

Hugo clapped his hands at Harold for the ball.

Alright, line up. Quit fucking around.

Everybody got serious. Joey hopped around looking for a gap to split, stepped back, slid over as everybody settled along the line. He stayed ready.

The neighborhood was full of children. Riding by on bicycles. Sitting on steps with ice cream cones. And playing games. Hopscotch frames chalked on the sidewalk, kids ran into the house to borrow sets of keys, or they used bottle caps to toss. They collected old newspapers for the rubber bands to braid into high jump ropes. Follow the leader along the curbs. Tag. Blob tag. Cap guns. Bubbles, small wands, big wands made from wire hangers.

Squirt guns. Water balloons. And they played ball in the street. Simple games of catch. Shared mitts. Ran between bases and avoided getting tagged out. Played strikeouts until a window got hit, twice. Tossed a football around and got games of touch going. Joey watched through the glass of his front door. His father took him by the hand and walked him to the sidewalk. *Go ahead, Joe. Play*. But he didn't join. He retreated against his father, who gently nudged him off the curb towards the game, *Joe, it's alright*, the boys ran amok in the street chasing after the ball, tugging shirttails, pushing a little too hard. They knew Joey. His father waved to them and left Joey there in between cars. One boy said hi. A few others waved. But Joey just watched. When they threw the ball high and far, Joey clapped and flapped his hands. When they screamed after a score, Joey hopped and flapped some more, skirted quickly on tiptoe along parked cars, hands fluttering furious. But he never played. He followed the game up and down the street but always stayed out of the boys' way. Joey mimicked them. He tossed the ball to a crossing boy. He waved someone to go deep and launched a pass. Joey caught a ball and danced up the street on high arches. Perfectly pantomimed. But he never joined the game. That was as close as Joey got. The sideline.

Hugo dropped back, ball high next to his ear. Joey put his hands on my shoulders and shed me. I fell forward, arms grasping at the air. He had a clear path to Hugo, who was like *oh shit* and spun to get away. Joey made a wide turn back, falling as he lunged and clipped Hugo's heel with a hand. Hugo stumbled and plopped to

40

the ground. The next play, Joey bull rushed over me and knocked the ball out of the air. Hugo jumped on it and Joey bellyflopped on top of him.

Tonio, blood, you gotta block him. He's a beast but you gotta stay in front of him. OK?

OK.

Awright?

Awright, Hugo.

Right on. Let's go.

Hugo clapped and I hiked him the ball. I threw my shoulder into Joey's gut and pushed as hard as I could. He moved with me, gave ground. He was light as a feather. Hugo flung the ball and Javier caught it for a big play. We jogged down the field.

What's your name?

Tonio.

Good block, Tonio.

Joey tapped me in the chest with his meaty fist. It thumped. I rubbed the spot.

Thanks. Nice jersey.

Earl Cooper, my favorite player.

Earl Cooper is your favorite?

Yeah. And I got 49 because I'm a 49er.

Joey gave me a thumbs up. He shook it at me and held it up until I responded in kind. He asked if I liked the Niners. Fuck yeah, I did. Everybody did. He gave me a double thumbs up.

We lined up and this time I jammed my hands into Joey's chest. He moved wherever I took him like we were dancing. But a few plays later, Joey shoved me straight into Hugo, falling on top of both of us. He was cool. And when he wanted, Joey dominated. Man.

It was later. No rain, but it was cold. The field got sloppy as we ran up and down. We were tired and wet. The game was about to be over soon. We felt it. But we still played hard. Hugo scrambled high knees and pointed toes and fired a laser to a crossing Harold. He caught the ball in stride and was behind everyone. Gone. Down the open field. But then out of nowhere, this dude Joey launched himself from the sideline and threw Harold to the ground by the shoulders. Harold fucking bounced, hard, his arms flew open and the ball shot into the air as he rolled several times over.

Ohhhh shit!

We all stopped to laugh. We couldn't help ourselves. Damn.

Joey wanted to be a football player for Halloween, so his father ordered him a 49er uniform out of a catalog complete with helmet and shoulder pads. Joey wore it every day until it was time to go trick-or-treating. He was all carnival head and clicking pads as he slid across the kitchen linoleum in his cleats like a cat on ice. *Joey, you're going to fall, darling* but he kept his motor going from the living room to the kitchen and back, streaking the hardwood and white linoleum alike, the football safely tucked away *Joey, the floors* the face mask didn't hide the earnestness in his face, the determination, he clawed the floors despite his mother's pleas.

42

He didn't hear them. His mother didn't care. It was too much fun to watch that enormous helmet bob around the house. His father carried his plastic pumpkin because Joey had to carry his football because he was wearing his 49er uniform. When he got to a doorstep and the neighbor asked the obligatory *and what are you supposed to be*, Joey darted across lawns or went deep down sidewalks, his mother close behind him. His father held the jack-o-lantern out for candy, explained *he wants to show you. He wants to show that he's a football player.* People were kind, equally impressed and confused, he certainly was a football player. They smiled wide and dropped extra candy, said *so cute.*

We were slow to line up, still chuckling about the play. Big Mario gripped Joey's hand like a homeboy and shook Joey, slapped him on the shoulder *good shit, young blood.* He lifted him and smacked him again. Talking about *that's my man.*

Hugo gave Joey a high five.

Yabalinski.

Who's Yabalinski?

This guy. Hugo held Joey affectionately by the scruff. He needs a fuckin leather helmet. Yabalinski, fullback from Notre Dame and shit.

My name's Joey.

Good shit, Joey. Hugo worked him over with swats, jabs and hooks. Joey covered up, at the same time nervous and pleased. He grinned bashful but his eyes blinked from the rowdy praise.

Aw fuck that. That's a flag, man.

Harold walked stiff-legged back to the group. He rubbed his hip, pulled his sleeve to check his elbow.

Fuuuuuck you, Harold. You're pissed cuz he threw you. Like a fuckin rag doll.

Fuck that. That's a penalty.

Harold checked his knee, licked his fingers and rubbed a spot. That's what Harold did. He complained. Every time we played, there was a moment where he stopped the game to bitch. Dudes stopped listening to him. That shit got old.

Never mind him. *Good stick, dude.* Joey grinned and nodded like a fanatic parrot.

The game was close. There was a lot of walking between plays, talking about what to do after the game. It was our ball on the 50. We ran it three times in a row so Hugo wanted to mix it up. He told Harold and Javier to set up wide and then crisscross over the middle. He'd find the open man. The rest of us stayed in and blocked.

Joey leaned over me. He breathed hard, twitched his fingers. Hugo clapped. I popped up but Joey didn't charge in. He backpedaled, elbows tight to his hips, his head on a swivel. Hugo rolled to his left, planted his foot and threw. Harold had broken free and waved for the pass, but Joey read the play all the way. He intercepted the ball and trucked through Harold, smashing into his chest and knocked him flat on his ass. Joey sprinted the other way. He was gone. Most of us quit after a few steps. Javier got close at the 5 but Joey somersaulted into the end zone. Touchdown.

Big Mario and them high-fived and clapped him on the

back. Joey smiled wide and gave a few awkward high fives back. The rest of us trotted in, talking about what we were up to next.

That's game. Who's up to go to the show?

Harold pushed through dudes, walked up on Joey and shoved him hard in the chest.

What's up then, what? Punk ass white boy!

Joey didn't understand. He froze. His arms stiff like naked branches. He trembled.

C'mon, chump. Now what?

Harold jabbed Joey in the shoulder. He got in his face and nudged him, huffing into his ear.

I scored a touchdown.

What'd you say, dumb ass?

I scored a touchdown.

Joey looked at the ground, chin tucked in. His eyes were frantic, frightened. His jaw hung open and clattered.

What the hell, Harold?

Man, fuck that. That's three fuckin times this punk ass bitch came at me. The first two were flags but you fucks ain't callin nothin. Forget you guys. This white boy ain't gonna punk me like that. So what's up?

C'mon, Harold. It's just a game.

Shut up, Tonio. I'm talkin to him.

I got in Harold's way.

Man, leave him alone.

Get your little ass out the way.

Harold grabbed me by the shoulders. I clutched his shirt

and pulled as hard as I could. We wrestled each other. He tried to throw me but I didn't let him go. We almost went down. Then Harold tightened his grip, pivoted and flung me aside. My feet flailed in the air. I was helpless, spun like a disc. I landed hard on my back, and my head hit the turf.

Hugo charged into Harold from the side and sent him stumbling. He almost regained his balance, but Hugo rushed again and made sure to knock Harold to the ground.

Fucker, you always gotta start shit. What the fuck? Tonio didn't do shit to you.

I got up slow, held the back of my head. I was a little woozy. It hurt like fuck but I played it off.

Harold got to his feet. Dusted himself. Dudes stood around all square. Ready. Harold didn't say anything. He checked his jaw. Kept his distance.

Fuck you guys.

Harold spat at us. Then he picked up the football and kicked it to the other end of the field. He sauntered off the field rubbing his chin. He flicked us off before he hopped the railing and walked to the exit, yelling inaudible cusses when he was far enough away.

The game broke up, it was over. Homeboys left a few at a time. They met up at the park before going to the movies. Or at Granada Market to play *Stargate*. No one moved to get the ball, so I went for it. I jogged ahead. Someone came up behind me. He put a heavy hand on my back.

Are you ok, Tonio?

Yeah, I'll be alright.

Joey put his finger in my chest.

You're tough. You're a tough guy. My buddy.

He gave me a strong-armed thumbs up, tapped my chest twice with his fist and ran ahead to get his football. He cut left then right practicing his moves, ready to get a game going again. Looking forward to next time. He backpedaled and waved at me to hurry up. I smiled. Fucking Joey. I ducked my head and hustled up the field as fast as I could to catch him.

8.

The laundromat isn't full by any means. I count four patrons. A white woman in black denim, jet black hair, thick black eyeliner, reads a magazine in a corner. A curvy woman, *hermosa*, sorts clothes out of a big *costal*. Her friend sits alone on a bench, kicking a leg and scrolling through his phone. I don't like the machines by the door because it gets cold, and I don't like being by the windows, all the people passing by and looking in, I imagine. I pick machines somewhere in the middle. Away enough. I lean my elbows on a folding table to read news on my phone. A dryer door slams across from me. I don't look up. Then coins click as they fall into a slot. *Esto es suyo?* The *hermosa* woman leans into my field of vision, curls her white-tipped fingers at me. I left my detergent on top of a machine. I move it and my bag and supplies to the table, scoot to the end. *Gracias.* I smile meekly. An older man, thin and dressed Tejano-style with a waxed and curled, way-too black mustache, is chatting *la hermosa* up, hovering over her. He's explaining songs that he's written, he's been writing lyrics since he was an adolescent, he kept them in a notebook that he rolled up and hid under his mattress, *verdad*, he was embarrassed to let anyone know that he wrote, that he had such ambitions, *tú sabes*. He poured over the pages in moments when his father and brothers were out in the fields, heads in a tractor, busy with a thresher, and he'd stolen away to get a drink of water, use the bathroom, whatever excuse got him back to the house, where he could scribble even for a few moments. His soul was in those pages. Thoughts he couldn't share with anyone. *Ay que triste,* she says, *que lástima,* what a pity, he must've been so alone holding all those thoughts in, she says as she sorts clothes. *Esto es suyo? Perdón.* I don't realize she's talking to me. *Yoo-hoo. Yoo-hoo. La hermosa* shakes a blue basket at me. I gesture no. *Yoo-hoo* is funny, I think. Who says that anymore.

The middle-aged Tejano leans in. She bumps him as she opens doors, loads clothes, pours detergent, brushes him out the way like it's nothing. He's on her hip, lithely steps around her, talks about all the years those songs spent tucked away, unread, unsung, unheard, waiting for the person meant for that unrequited love. One day, he is going to meet her, that special woman. Maybe she's the one he's been looking for. He pulls a black bandana from a shirt pocket and he sings to her, a bolero, but she wants no part of it. *Ay no, por favor… hay gente. Not in front of people.* She caps a bottle of bleach and walks away. He follows her, explains the song, he wrote it for a girl he knew in his *rancho*, she always wore a pretty yellow dress and he saw her pass on the road each day as she went to the mill accompanied by her sister. He smiled at her but she never smiled back, he said hello but they never spoke until one day she looked at him and he understood. He cleaned up that afternoon when the workday was done and went to her house with a handful of posies. *Buenas tardes, me llamo José Rogelio Ruiz y Picasso.* And that was all he was allowed to say before the father told him to never return, he was never going to be welcomed there. Young José Rogelio didn't understand until one day he learned the story about the feud between his father and the girl's father. They would never, could never meet. *Por favor, Romeo y Julieta Ruiz y Picasso, I know that old story.* It's been done before. *La hermosa* spins away, drums the table with her shiny fingernails. Her very big *nalgas* are propped in his face. Nothing flirty or teasing. It's more like *talk to the ass, no me jodas vos.*

Don José Rogelio holds the bandana in both hands. Maybe she prefers to hear a song without exposition, and he sings, serenades her in the middle of the laundromat. She doesn't sit still for it. She busies herself between machines and dryers, and finally turns to her friend who's been listening all this time from the bench, scrolling and bouncing his knee. *Ayudame, Romel. Help me.* He covers his mouth to hide his smirk. *Jefe, the truth is that you can't appreciate the song in here, don,* the acoustics are dreadful and he's afraid the don is wasting such a beautiful song in those dismal conditions. The humming is drowning him out. Romel holds a finger in the air, pauses to listen. Perhaps there's a better time and place. Don José Rogelio agrees, Romel's correct that a bolero deserves a place with adequate décor and mood, so he'll content *la hermosa* with a *corrido* instead. He taps his foot and slaps his thigh, and she throws her hands up, *por dios, no*, and flees. She sits on the bench with Romel but quickly moves to the vending machine and acts like she wants something, runs a finger up and down the glass wondering out loud about a candy bar or chips or cookies. *Romel, quieres una Coca? We can share if you want.* Don José Rogelio Ruiz y Picasso keeps on her heels, a hand to his chest and lightly touches her shoulder. *La hermosa* recoils *ay, muchas gracias, ya basta, gracias. Pero no gracias.* She storms away and stands in front of a washer. She crosses her arms, cocks her telenovela hips as clothes turn in the glass. Hat in hand, the Tejano asks her name. Úrsula. He introduces himself, formally, and invites her out, he wants to take her to dinner later. *Gracias* but she's busy, waves a hand like *with all this*. Tomorrow night then. *Ay no*, she's busy, too. This week isn't a good week for *encuentros*. He trails her as she pushes a cart to a folding table. The Tejano persists. At least allow him to sing her one more song, Úrsula reminds him of a classic José Alfredo Jimenez song and he sings the first bars into her ear but she stops him short.

Oh my god, por favor, Jose Alfredo Jimenez que aburrido. How boring.

Then una de …

No, no gracias, ya me cansé.

Úrsula shakes her arms exasperated. Well, then he'll be better prepared the next time he sees her. Don José Rogelio will return soon. *Sí, como no* we'll be waiting for you. *Que le vaya bien*.

Don José Rogelio bows and backs out. He gives a final wave with his hat through the window and disappears. Úrsula glances at me. I fold my underwear carefully, make neat stacks of five. Then I put socks into pairs. I make a game out of it like Concentration. Úrsula dumps clothes on the table and begins to sort jeans from tops from leggings from sweats.

¿Esta calceta es suya?

She shows me the sock. It's covered in animals. No. I smile shy.

Porque I saw it close to your things. I thought it must be yours.

I raise my eyebrows, no. I fold my pants.

People leave their things everywhere. Qué barbaridad.

I keep folding, carefully line up the creases on my pants.

Úrsula snaps a pair of jeans, hangs them over the cart. She snaps a few more pairs.

I think I know you.

I mouth, *no sé.*

Hmm… She taps her lip, thoughtful.

Úrsula holds up a pair of jean shorts, a small pair. Small. She folds them quickly and moves on.

I don't offer anything and the conversation dies. She calls out to Romel about what they're going to do for dinner. She's starving. He doesn't answer. He's laughing at a video. *Romel, dije que tengo hambre,* she says. Úrsula swings a bedazzled hoodie in his direction. She's hungry, damn it, but she doesn't want to cook. And, god no, neither does he. It's too late to go to the store and figure what to buy, and *además no quiero.* She's tired and frustrated and done, *pero cansada.* Romel suggests why don't they go to la Yajaira's. She always has rice and beans, fried chicken *por lo menos.*

I know who Úrsula is. She's the hippy, *hermosa* tranny that lives in the building next to mine. We come and go like folks on Mission do, we know each other but we don't, we become part of the daily circulation, the rhythms of the barrio, its faces, single-minded in the morning, consternated and anguished to make it home in the evening. I've seen her many times. She breezes by in pastel scrubs, yellow, pink, blue, green, and a simple leather pocketbook. No makeup, just light powder. Days off, she walks a tiny dog while she eats an ice cream or *elote.* Úrsula's steps are abrupt like her pet, but she doesn't hurry, takes her time to eat, think. She must see me in the neighborhood, too.

A trio, decked in white hats and white boots and guitars strapped across their backs, stops outside to smoke. Oh god, Úrsula hopes out loud that they don't come in. *Tranquila*, Romel says, they're only smoking. *Traumatizada.* He chuckles. *Pobre viejo.* He was sweet though. Úrsula maddogs Romel. Mouths, *no jodas*.

I'm almost done. All I have left are my button up shirts.

How do I know you? No sé de donde. But I know you.

I shrug.

Romel says that la Yajaira just sent a text. She's making *indio viejo*. If they're going to be late, she says for them to bring a bottle of wine, something nice, like fifteen dollars. *Ay, sí, me muero de hambre. I'm starving and sick of laundry*. Úrsula tells Romel that he better help her, *mamón*, if he wants to eat soon. *Ideay, dije ayudame,* she says and stamps her foot, so get up already, *jodido*, and help. *Me muero*. She puts her wrist to her brow, sighs deep.

We kinda met once.

I was at the bar by myself. Typically, I made a simple dinner, a salad with fish or chicken, if not then whole grain bread and things like figs, blueberries, green olives, walnuts, cherry tomatoes, gouda cheese; I tried to be healthy, I needed to be after my doctor recommended that I go on medication for high blood pressure. Fuck, I was too young for that, I thought. Or, I could try to deal with it on my own. She said no cold cuts, *OK*, no fried foods, *son of a bitch, no queso frito and maduros*, no bad fats, *a la puchica, my sour cream,* and no pork, *motherfucker!* Walking helped. I ran some. Did pull-ups and push-ups. It worked. I lost weight. My blood pressure lowered. I felt better. I kept it up, like my doctor said. But there was still something not quite right. I thought about it for weeks as I walked around the lake in the dark, predawn; as I walked over the ruined foundation of the Sutro Baths at sunset. Then one afternoon I was sitting at my kitchen table over a bowl of hot oatmeal. It reminded me of when I was little. My grandmother waited at the church hall for food every Tuesday. She brought home boxes of oatmeal that she made with butter and salt. It was creamy with a few lumps. I loved it. I ate it in front of the TV. Then I remembered my stepfather yelling at me, what did he say about eating in the living room, I never listened like always, that's why he said he was sending me away to an *academia,* a reform school. Because I was *malcriado.* He threatened me. He was going to do it. But it didn't frighten me. I got angry. *Estoy bravo* was what I told my grandmother when she found me pouting in the closet. It drove me mad that he thought he could send me away without telling anyone. I shouted, *no you can't, no you can't* each time he said it. I'd run to the bathroom and I'd spit. I told mama what he said, that he said it a lot. Because I was bad. Mama didn't get angry. Her face was sad, her eyes weren't bright like they usually were. She said not to listen. But I didn't know how to do that, he said it all the fucking time when mama wasn't there and it made me so fucking mad, I sat and banged my head against the wall because I couldn't make him stop, there was nothing I could do except feel *bravo, mama, I don't want to be, I'm not bad; he is.* It wasn't true, mama said. She pulled out a small square notebook and drew a tic-tac-toe frame and we played. She let me go first and I won each time. She drew a line across another page and handed me the pen. I drew a sun. She drew a penguin. I laughed and scratched an umbrella on a beach. Then mama wrote *mi pansonsito, yo te quiero. I will always love you. The truth*, she said. She handed me back the pen. I could do the same. Whatever I wrote in the notebook was true. But I wanted him to stop. Mama said don't worry, she'd take care of it. So, when that fucker said mean things to me, I drew and wrote in my notebook. I did so until the day I didn't have to anymore. Anymore.

I was sad.

I had been for a long time, so on top of building healthy habits, I found happy habits, go to the movies, browse used bookstores, find new walks to explore the city. I wanted to be healthy, but my dinner also made me happy, I ate, watched TV, stopped to write in square notebooks I kept, sometimes I got ideas, a good idea I thought, I might use later, a story maybe. With the TV on, I read, fell asleep on the sofa with a book on my chest, happy. But tonight, I was antsy in the apartment, and decided to head to the corner for drinks. I wasn't looking for company. I was good listening to music. I liked to hear the voices. I was content with the bartender checking in with me and sharing casual chatter. It was enough to be around a few other people.

A booth was full of young ladies who fêted a bride, and another gathering of people shot pool in the back. Folks were spread over the bar. The jukebox played a familiar set. It was a good night.

I was alone at the end of the bar, except for a napkin over a glass. I sipped whisky and soda, glanced casually at the TV. A stool screeched. It was Úrsula, who uncovered the glass and sipped the drink through a tiny red straw. She was with a friend, same impossible curves but shorter. They were loud, threw their heads back to cackle. A dude walked over and stood between them. He introduced himself, offered his hand, which they took and shook ladylike, very formal. He waved to catch the bartender's eye.

Úrsula sat up straight on her stool, her *nalgas* popping out. Ridiculous. New drinks came and dude raised his glass and clinked carefully, sure to look them each in the eye. He talked to them both but little by little he got closer to Úrsula, touched her knee with his drink hand. Her friend got up and flipped through the jukebox catalog. Dude slid a stool against Úrsula. He was animated, circled his hands in the air as he spoke, careful not to spill his drink. He leaned into Úrsula's ear, *no, da cosquillas* and she swatted at him like a fly, he smiled, laughed and went back in, she let him, her shoulders trembling until she couldn't stand anymore and burst out laughing, *da cosquillas*. He tapped her knee, *con permiso,* and got up to use the bathroom. Úrsula swayed to the music, sipped through the tiny red straw and then Gloria Gaynor, "I Will Survive" came on, but the Celia Cruz version and Úrsula leapt off her stool, *chocho,* high-fived her homegirl and they danced together, an arm around the other's waist. Úrsula stabbed the air as she sang along with Celia, *yo viviré, yo viviré.* Her friend returned to the bar for a drink. The bartender poured a round of shots, from the dude in the bathroom, he signaled. Úrsula toasted her homegirl and they downed the shots. *Uy hijueputa*, it was strong and her friend needed to sit.

Úrsula stayed up, a hand against the jukebox. She kept the empty shot glass raised. Her homegirl applauded, cheered. Úrsula sang, *ya me verás, que soy feliz, un nuevo mundo de ilusión se ha abierto para mi,* and then she moved into a talking blues kind of thing, she recalled Nicaragua and how she missed her patria, it'd been 18 years since she left and she wanted to return, had hope *pero desgraciadamente* she couldn't now, not with this new trans-hating, *gente*-hating *hijo de la gran puta* in the White House, no one was going anywhere but she had hope, she'd outlast that *fucker hijueputa,* she'd return to embrace her sweet mother and father, they'd be so happy to see how she continued to succeed, thrive, flourish, *no jodas,* thanks to them. Úrsula had perfected who she was in *el US* but she didn't discover herself here. She knew damn well who she was in Granada, *everyone knew, jueputa, desde la Oficina Chamorro, 20 varas al norte, humildemente I was born under a zinc sheet roof, de lámina*, and her father took her in his arms and blessed her, *mil bendiciones esa noche,* and gave her his name, and he began to dream *all the things I would have in life that he couldn't have, I wasn't going to suffer like they did, I was born under a special moon and God had big plans for me, the moon had never been bigger in the sky y tenía que ser enorme para recibirme, papa gave me what he could, estudios, libros, uniformes, he taught me what he could, his business, how to paint the billboard advertisements along la Carreterra Masaya, swift strokes, bold, precise.* Úrsula could still feel the air rise up and her legs swinging as they sat 15 meters above the ground, and her father talked to her about fishing in the lake when the job was done, he was taking her fishing, they'd catch handsome fish, eat and drink and talk; he was proud, even when Úrsula let her hair grow once she finished her *bachillerato* and took a course in Managua to learn how to draw blood. Soon after she completed her studies, she found work in a clinic and her shifts were days long and she was away often. When she was home, *chocho*, how she loved to go down to *el turismo* along the big lake and feel the wind blow in off the rippling water as she ate steamed turtle eggs, *tostones, chicharrón*, and danced and danced and danced, her thick curls gathered on top of her head to beat the heat. Her father was still proud, even when.

Úrsula twirled, wound her hips up and down, sang like she owned the song. Dude was back from the bathroom. He toasted Úrsula, too. He danced with her, placed a hand on her waist. She lifted her head to the ceiling, swayed and raised her arms high, then let them drop graceful. Dude slid his hand down, and she knocked it away. He smiled and gave her a good smack on the *nalgas*.

Hey, she stuck a finger in his face. Soy una dama, oíste. A lady. You respect me, hijueputa. You hear? Qué te pasa?

Dude backed off hands up, grinning. Úrsula got back into the song. But dude was bold, no shame, and swatted her ass again.

A la gran puta!

She swung at his head. Dude grabbed her around the waist. Úrsula pushed against his chest and freed herself. She reared back, but in her windup, she knocked a drink across the bar. It sprayed me in the eyes, stung, and I half stumbled off my stool.

Ay perdón!

Úrsula tried to help me, dabbed my shirt with a napkin but dude yanked her away. She yelled an ugly *motherfucker!* Suddenly, her homegirl punched his ear, beat him hard on the back. Úrsula twisted loose and cussed him out while homegirl continued to beat his ass. *Hijo de las cien mil putas*, she screamed, and then seamlessly, she joined the song again. Her hands framed her face dramatic, the glow of the jukebox washed her in *girasol* while homegirl roughed up the handsy dude, drove him to the door. Úrsula performed, her hands interpreting the lyrics while the scuffle backed her up. The bartender came around and helped her homegirl take the fuckhead dude outside. The pool game stopped a moment to see what the commotion was, but then went back to shooting, balls clacking and falling into holes. Show was over.

The next morning, I was hella late for work. I put on the same pants, a clean shirt and ran out. As I exploded onto the sidewalk, a dog started yapping. It startled the shit out of me. Úrsula bent over to scold the dog, *malo*. It hopped frantic and she stamped her foot, *no Fernando, qué te pasa?* Fernando circled her, growled from behind her ankles.

Perdón.

I gestured it was no problem.

Me llamo Úrsula.

I already knew. Soy Antonio.

I wondered why that name. A tía, her grandma, someone

else she cared about. Not Nicaragüense like Gioconda. Or Daisy. It was theatrical. A statement. The dog had calmed down. She crouched to give him a treat, rubbed his ear.

Bueno, I have to go.

She walked away, heels click-clacking. She held her head high, shook the hair from her face when the wind kicked up. Her big hips didn't swish. She glided away like a little sailboat. Steady.

That was the one time we ever met.

I'm coming to an intersection and I see Úrsula. She's jaywalking across South Van Ness, swings her *hermosura* proudly. A large full-cab pickup rushes towards the crosswalk honking at her, furious, pissed, continuous. She strolls, *tranquila*, doesn't hurry to the curb, a small boutique shopping bag in hand. She does a little hair flip, all cool, even though she is wrong for walking into traffic, but cool. The truck roars past her plentiful *tepalcuanas* all fucking mad and it almost clips her, horn blaring, middle finger extended. Úrsula doesn't trip. She adjusts the wide gold belt around her impossibly tiny waist. Unaffected. She smiles, coy, and then gives a subtle wave to an adoring public as she steps onto the curb, safe.

9.

It's been raining torrents for days, approaching a week and people are trippin. Oh my god. This is so strange, they say. It's climate change, they say. Like the fires are raging more and more out of control each year. Oh my god, my eyes burned and it was awful to breathe. They couldn't believe it. Everyone wore masks during all those days in the purple zone. That strange, awful light. Each year gets worse.

But it hardly ever rains like this.

I remember fires when I was a kid. A few. So far away. Tucked in pockets of California I never saw. An ancient forest maybe, which made it sound sad. But the trees recovered. And the fire never touched me.

The rain touched every day of winter though. It rained in April, too. And July. These people are trippin. They don't know that it's supposed to rain so much. It's best that it does.

A handful of people stand in the Walgreens entrance waiting for the light to turn green. Instinctively, they huddle together to protect themselves from the cold.

The runoff surges against the curb and pours through the sewer grate. The water can't pass as quickly as it comes so it collects and partially floods the corner. A thin man with a thick wiry beard stands in that gutter, deliberately. He holds a tall can of energy drink high in the air, euphoric, face to the sky catching chilled drops on his grimy cheeks. He hikes up his baggy pants to avoid the water, but it's old habit because they're always falling. He's immersed. His feet are set together to block the flow and the water rushes around his ankles. He moves his toes up and down in the brown runoff, curious, shifting his feet so the water crests, slows, spills over his shoes. It's a subtle dance, innocent joy. He's like a child. He's celebrating. He's completely happy.

They don't take notice, but the people in the entrance bunch closer together, looking for comfort, their wet faces jumpy for the light to change.

10.

I walk the streets at odd hours, late.

I forget why I'm out at all. I'm not alone. I can't be even if I wanted. A couple stands on a corner staring into their phones. Others sing and talk too loud about nothing, really, nothing happened that night at the bar. Just bullshit yelled into the hollow night. Fuckheads. It's also the time some folks got to work. Inside a closed business, a cleaning woman bends over in an awkward position, reaches for something just beyond fingertips, under a stool, a sponge mop leaning against a piano, the whole scene crammed into a picture window.

This is how people live. This is how people have always lived. Stooped, moving quick, mechanical. Hardly seen.

11.

An old man spreads his sleeping bag outside the school on a square cut from the building next to an emergency exit, he has two walls for shelter, he sits crisscross facing the school, his back to walking traffic. He's bald, white tufts of hair above his ears, his reddened scalp and neck dry and cracked, flaky. He keeps a tidy gray blanket folded over his lap, his notebooks stacked neatly on a corner of his bedding, and hunches over his writing. Protected by his broad striped back, he composes, mouths words as they come to mind, the scribbles and scratches audible, the script clear, neat, minute, he stops to read his work aloud, make corrections, strike words, entire lines, and reads them again. He falls in a visible rhythm. His days, he scavenges more notebooks, pads, and books, tossed paperbacks; he's content, he's well, a container of food next to his notebooks, a loaf of sliced bread if he's lucky, he'll scrape the bottom of the takeout with his plastic fork during a break, review his work as he chews. When he writes, he has purpose, is quiet and calm and pays no one any mind; he's not a drunk, never high, doesn't bother folks. He writes, stops only to roll up his bedding, which makes him angry and he growls at the officers, but moves to the opposite corner when they order him. Then he carefully unrolls his bedding, stretches out on his belly like a grade schooler to continue his writing. When the sidewalk is washed, he throws his blanket over his notebooks, and lays over them. The old man tucks his books carefully under his body, flattens himself so they're protected as the hose sprays everywhere, soaks his ankles, bruised and yellowish. He shivers, waits for the worker to guide the filth into the gutter, the generator droning loud as ever. The old man talks to himself, whispers to his books, they're ok, he squints hard and presses his forehead to the cold cement, recites to remember, to keep every single word intact.

He arranges children's books neatly along the corner. If people want a book, they can leave money in a cup and take the title they like. He isn't watching for customers. Obviously, he's too busy writing. People will find what they like if anything. Everyone is on the honor system.

12.

The lights were glowing on the altar, enough candles lit for all the souls and a bit of hope. Her friends stayed a while longer to light one more candle and say a last unrehearsed prayer. My grandmother waited outside. She fell right there. Never opened her eyes again.

I complained about going to church every Sunday. Each time, abuelita heard me but made me go because it was important that I went, she said. Because I was young.

But you never go, abuelita.

Ah, I'm already old. *A mi ya no me sirve ir.* It does me no good to go. God isn't thinking about me. *Tú sí.*

So, I went because abuelita told me to. And you couldn't ever say no to abuelita.

13.

The lights are on at 4:00 in the morning. The **For Sale** sign is posted above the narrow garage. Three immaculate white flats for sale just off the corner of 23rd and Mission.

This could be you.

The halogen lights attract the human moths that bar hop the hip Mission scene. Someone might take notice as a friend holds their hair to the side.

14.

I told mama I was going to the liquor store across the street because it had new video games, *Popeye* and *Millipede*. I pushed through folks crowding at the corner. I was a little kid and on one ever moved aside for little kids. Then I saw why they had crowded. I nearly stepped on him. He had a triangular gash in the middle of his forehead, blood filling the furrows of his brow and trailing into his eyes. He was marked like an undesirable. His hands pressed over his abdomen. His shirt was quickly soaking up blood and it pooled on his belly. He cried loud and sharp:

> I been stabbed.
> He stabbed me.
> He stabbed me! oh god.

His voice was gravelly. It was like a needle in a groove when the song was over. I was surprised that he was conscious. Eyes wide open looking up into the overcast sky, blood bubbling between his fingers. I thought he would fade and gradually grow quiet. He didn't. He only got louder.

People surrounded him, gawked, but they did nothing. No one scrambled to get help or even knelt next to him to provide first aid, no one told him it was alright, not to worry because everything would be fine. No one did anything. It was quiet, except for his panicked yelping. I lost sight of him among the huddled bodies. People moved me back to get better looks. Started guessing about what happened, why someone stabbed the man.

Talked about if you fuck around, that was what you got. He kept crying out, wounded and confused and scared, his wails amplified, harmonized by the sirens as the police and an ambulance pulled up to the curb.

15.

The rain poured over the large square windshield. I liked to sit up front behind the driver. It was like sitting in front of a big silver screen and the street rolling up was a movie. Lots of times I had to get up for old ladies or a woman carrying a baby and stroller. Once in a while, a person in a wheelchair. But many times I got to sit and watch, my feet swinging as the bus sped through green lights and rolled to stops. Up front was better when it rained. When it rained, the bus loaded with people and then all the windows fogged up. It was good because you could draw on the glass, faces with big noses and missing teeth, birds, hearts pierced by arrows, tic-tac-toe, dookie. But I always wanted to see outside. I was a curious kid, looked over counters, stuck my nose between elbows. I needed to see what was passing by me, what was ahead.

The rain beat on the windshield in sheets that splashed water across the glass. The storm was jazzy, tapped the high hat, free beat, swept the skins with wire brushes, and rose into a blind wash. For several moments, we drove not knowing what was ahead of us, if someone took a chance to jam across the street, or a bicyclist inched along the side. We trusted the driver, everybody brave. It was exciting driving into the storm. I craned to see over the driver's shoulder. The long wipers swept the water away, rhythmic, worked like a drum. It was a dark morning, everything moved slow. People were late. The traffic built ahead, the red taillights glowing and the bus slowing down, stopped sudden, everyone lurching forward together. I could see the people at the corner stops, stuffed under the shanty shelters and blooming along the curb in black umbrellas, plastic bubbles, one giant red canopy. They took turns to see if the bus was coming. We were coming. *Hold on.* We were on our way.

The bus creeped forward. I watched the traffic light go from red to yellow to green. Brakes exhaled but then a neighborhood dude, coatless and yelling mad in the downpour, stepped in between the cars and held us up. The driver honked, blared. The mad dude scratched his jagged crown and whisked his other arm, stiff with rage. We missed the chance to go. Again, the traffic light was back at red and we had to start over. The driver deflated in his seat. The 14 Mission was already a long ass ride from the top of the hill in Daly City through the entire Mission and all the way downtown to the Embarcadero and the troubled bay. In the rain, it was forever.

Finally, we got a green light. The crowd at 16th Street pushed to meet the bus. The folks crowded onto the front steps, the doors barely unfolded. They reached for the frame, and talked to each other as they stepped in unison, urged each other to get on, hurry it up, *jovero*, it was fucking raining. They massed around the entrance like ants, probing and elbowing. Eventually, with no option, they had to enter in single file. A couple of doñas, heavily padded in coats and shawls and bufandas, climbed the three steps like escalating Everest, taking a breath after each step and prepared their grips for the next one up. The doña behind chided the one ahead, playful, *cuidado no te vayas a caer, you'll take us all, pobrecitos whoever's behind us, they're waiting, qué vergüenza, ha ha ha, one more little step and we are safe.* Obviously, I had to give up my seat.

I made my way back, head forward into hips. I said excuse me repeatedly as I pushed between bodies clogging the middle, folks never went all the way back, they needed to be close to the exit to make their stop. I forced my way to a pair of empty seats just past the back door. I took the window seat, wiped the condensation. Folks continued climbing onto the bus, more calm now, finding seats and making way, a bit at a time. *Transfer. Transfer, please.* The request was too loud, unnecessary, and it startled folks, unsettled them. It was an old white woman that plowed steadily through people, barking, down the aisle. She looked bad. Noxious. Repellent. She was potbellied in a white tank top, pallid congealed arms moving persons out of her way. Ruddy, bulbous nose. Hair wet and stringy. She was nasty.

I couldn't look away. I stared at her as she moved towards me, unblinking, struck. Then I realized the seat next to me was empty. I looked down then up and down again as she got closer. I thought *holy shit.* I didn't want her to sit next to me. But I didn't move. I was panicked. Then I caught the old woman's eye. She noticed my dread. I scrambled to get out, but she was quicker, swung her big bulky hips around and forced me back into the seat. Shoved me in. We plopped down together. She scowled at me. She knew I wanted to get out. She knew I wanted to get far away from her. I tried to climb over her lap and she brushed me back with her thick arm. She was strong like a man. Her arm was stiff like a heavy tree limb. Fucking frontier strong. I tried again. She pushed me down. That made me mad that she could push me down. Fuck her, fucking white lady. My face flushed, I felt myself get red all over. A sweat washed over me. Motherfuck that fucking old white lady. I clambered frantically, frenzied, over her again and she threw me back down with both arms, pushed me down a second time to make sure I stayed put in the seat.

Excuse me.

What?

Say excuse me.

She stunk of alcohol. Her skin was rough, dried and scaly like a reptile. She bowed her arm out to block me, locked it against the seat in front of us. It pressed across my collarbone. Her hot breath came in quick puffs, exerted, grunting.

Excuse me.

Say excuse me, *please*.

Excuse me, please.

She lowered her arm and leaned back and I pushed past her, shoved her somewhere on her doughy body, angry, pissed that she forced me to sit, fucking angry that she kept me until she wanted to let me go. Fuck you, fucking old white lady, I thought as I pulled my legs out, elbowed and brushed past her to the back of the bus.

I found a seat among the three that faced the aisle. I knelt to look out the window. Really, I was hiding. I folded my arms across the backrest and buried my face in them. I didn't cry but my cheeks felt damp, my eyes did water. I fingered the foggy glass. Papa was across from me, my brother and sister tucked next to him.

Tonio…

I faced him, still kneeling.

Make sure to stay close to me.

I didn't answer. I was still angry. Fucking old lady. I sat on my haunches, drew tiny circles all over. Then I rose up to open the window. I pulled on the lock to slide the glass but it didn't budge. I grabbed the lock with both hands and leaned back, pulled with my body. Papa told me to stop. Don't open the window. It was raining outside, and cold.

I didn't listen. I kept pulling. I was so mad. I saw the ads lined along the roof of the bus as I continued to pull, as hard as I could. I read each one, the poster directly above me was about a car. A sports car. Red and only two bucket seats. New. Racy. Fuego.

16.

Uva was as strong as an ox. He was immovable once he picked his spot to post up. He had strength like to blow up a hot water bottle like a party balloon until it burst. Franco Columbu and shit. Uva was a boa in the forest. He stood so still he blended in with the liquor ads and concert posters and graffiti hit up on free wall spaces. He wasn't a big drinker, took a reluctant swig, mostly listened to our nonsense, *chisme*, called out our bragging, *he doesn't even realize what a stupid ass he's being saying that shit,* and made intermittent remarks about hip-hop, the first tape so-and-so put out, B-side gems no one talks about, *that's just a bite from a Prince song and shit, it's sick how the beat's laid over but it's a sample, stupid fuckers don't know,* his points made one-armed, chopping, his other hand perpetually tucked in his parka pocket.

We were on Uva's steps one night, right. Alvaro messed with the cassette in the boom box, flipping it over, rewinding and fast forwarding to find a song, *your gonna fuck it up, dude,* but he held up a hand to hold on a minute, *just let the tape play and shit, bestia, the whole album is cool anyway.* Alvaro chuckled and kept fucking with the cassette, Dave reaching out, buzzed, and swiping at his elbow, a knee to get his attention, went through me cuz I was between them, *dude, dude, hey blood,* trying to tell his story about the party at Gloria's, *listen up, it was like this, right, like this,* fucking Charles/Backtrax was spinning, so was Walter, we knew him, right, the music was bumping, sick right, and the garage was packed, there were hella girls, fine ass fuck, hella thick, but nobody was dancing, all these fools posted up and nobody was asking girls to dance, so Dave was like fuck it, smoothed his hair and walked across the floor. He saw this one girl, kinda cute, smile all shy, she was kinda moving side to side, snapped her fingers, so he asked if she wanted to dance, *she was just waiting for me to ask her, blood,* Alvaro nodded, *for real,* turned the stereo up, and Dave went on about how they were dancing close, he was getting at her, talking, throwing game, little breaths on her neck cuz she was hella short, *you feel me,* and she was cool, they were dancing, his hands on her hips, she was like caressing his neck and shoulders and shit, Uva was there, we could ask him. *This dude was dancin like he was socking her in the ribs.* Alvaro and me cracked up, he spilled a bit of his 40 oz, drank quick to clean it up and offered me the bottle but I was like *I'm cool,* I was buzzing enough already, I just wanted to listen to the story. Alvaro took another drink and passed the bottle to Dave, *but I was dancing though, right, not like these punk asses standing around*, he was at least doing good with a lady on the dance floor. *Dancing? All this dude was doing was moving his arms like a robot with low ass batteries and his face was hella red like he was dancing salsa and shit.* Alvaro and me busted up, we were rolling, talking about Uva called him salsa blood, I felt my cheeks, they were hella warm. Dave set the 40 on the top step. Then he shoved me hard and stood up.

What's up then, blood? Do something. I been looking for a reason for hella long cuz I know you can't step to me. Anything you do, I know I can take it. I won't even feel it.

Dave stood over me. He had a thick *chancho*, pig head and stocky body. He was fat but solid. At school, he surprised dudes when he bench-pressed 225lbs five times, bounced the bar easily off his chest, short arms pumping like pistons. He surprised dudes cuz he was a little over five feet. But he was built perfect for the bench. Nothing else, that was all.

I rose up and faced him. Shaky but I wasn't a punk. Dave moved in, snorted in my face. But Uva yanked him away. Dave flew and slammed against the wall. Alvaro jumped up immediately and got in between us, too.

Motherfucker, don't ever come at Tonio like that, bitch. I'll beat your ass! Gonna pull that shit on my steps. Man, I will beat your chump ass.

Dave straightened himself up, but Uva gave him another stiff jab into the wall. We all froze a moment and waited to see what was up. Dave was slumped against the wall, not moving.

We gave him our back and sat down on the steps, Alvaro fucking with the tape again and Uva telling him to quit that shit, the tape was gonna get stuck in the fucking mechanisms and snag, just let it play, especially side 2, there were three songs on that side that should've been singles, they didn't even have videos, *for real*, but they should've made the Hot 100. *Quit it, you mental case.* Alvaro took a big drink of the 40, offered me some but I was still cool, still buzzing. Uva went on about lyrics, how one song fucked with meter and rhyme scheme, got away from ABAB CDCD and about to turn hip-hop out, some new shit, but you gotta let the fuckin tape alone so you can hear the shit, goofy ass. Alvaro laughed, was finally like *alright*, and set the stereo aside, turned it up.

Dave asked if there was any more 40. Alvaro slid the beer to him without looking. Dave killed the bottle and said we needed to put in for another 40. He tugged a bill from his pants pocket. He went on about before. The party, right. He did end up getting that girl's number though. For real, he wasn't lying.

17.

He said his name with a shy giggle. I looked up and noticed his eyes. They were large, dark, expressive with thick brows that bowed over them and made him look quizzical. The woman asked his name again, she didn't catch it the first time, love. He cleared his throat, swallowed. His grin widened, filled the space. *My name is Henry.* He said it well-rehearsed, his accent sanded down after twenty-odd years of practice. He took a breath first like a school boy, maybe a patient teacher in his mind, *Henry, it's OK,* urging, even though English made him uneasy, made him shake his head at the unnatural syllables. Didn't matter. He wanted to be understood. So he repeated himself, *Henry.* I remembered him, that lively stare, that silly grin. He was forever smiling, happy ass. I knew that dude.

Henry didn't want to go. *I want to stay with you, mama.* No. He was going to go to live with his Tía Chayo in the States, he had to go. *No, mama. I'm staying here, no me voy.* He bubbled, began to toe tap, *I'm staying, mama. – clap clap clap –* He flashed his clumsy, burlesque smile, rubbed circles over her shoulders as he hugged his mother loosely, arranged himself into the perfect position to give her the fatal embrace, the one that would change her mind, *mama, I want to be with you, mama. I want to stay.* Salvadora looked away as she held her son, Henry had no filter, he was love unadulterated, he didn't know any other way to be, why would anyone not want to feel loved, *a hello does no harm,* his glee was contagious, infectious, he thought everyone was a friend, indiscriminate, and so he had to leave. There were no friends. Not anymore. He'd get hurt if he stayed. Too gentle. Too warm. Too agreeable. His love would be wasted in Nicaragua. *Hijo, I love you. – Then I can stay, sí sí sí.* Salvadora held Henry warmly, tender, noted how tall he had become, *like his father,* she thought, Henry was a whole head taller than her, which she didn't want to accept, that he was grown, because it was more reason for him to go, to leave her arms, she couldn't keep him anymore. He was the right age, the right size. She stroked his back, patted him between the shoulder blades the way she did when he was a toddler, so playful, restless when she needed to put him down to nap, fidgety, he squirmed in her arms, *tranquilo, hijo, za za za sleep* she cooed because she was spent. *I'm tired, hijo.* But he'd wriggle free.

He always wanted to do everything. She'd show him how to crack an egg without breaking the yolk, stir the gallo pinto (his favorite), help roll the pestle over Bisabuela Mercedes' ancient stone slab to grind chiles congos. After breakfast, there was a respite, time for her chores as Henry jumped puddles, poked a stick in milky gray water, drew a big circle in the dirt to shoot his chibolas, his marbles, a Cat's eye in his cheek as he steadied his eye over the masher, Salvadora shouting, *Henry, no*, he could choke before he scattered his marbles into the street, *Henry, no*, so he moved inside, toy cars, tops, jacks, suddenly, drop everything and dart into the kitchen with untied shoes, *ideay mama, my shoe, look ideay;* he untied them on purpose and acted surprised. He pleaded to bounce on her knee. She turned him over and tickled his back as she sang *sana sana sana culito de rana.* Then shaved ice to cool off heavy with syrup, piña o tamarindo, Salvadora nibbled his fingers when he asked her to taste. Finally, *ya Henry*. No more. She needed to put him down. There was wash to do, or something, *siempre algo*.

Salvadora sang to him *duermase mi niño, que ahí viene el coyote,* leaned over and covered his eyes and shushed. Instead, he kicked the bedsheet off, *Henry, it's time* – *no, mama,* he was hungry, drumming his belly, so she got up to make tortillas. He watched them puff up, helped stoke the fire and stoke the fire and stoke the fire, *ya hijo, you're wasting firewood.* Henry liked to sweep the ashes out and watch them pour onto the ground. He ate and she watched him, admired his big eyes. He was so funny, about wearing his leather boots without socks, *no, never,* the way he fluttered his fingertips over his mouth, how he liked to watch a feather fall, or string, or leaves. All of it bliss.

You'll be fine with Tía Chayo, hijo.

Henry smushed his cheek against his mother's and squeezed her, *do you love me, mama,* tickled her waist, *yes, you do, you don't want me to go*, but she took his hands away, swallowed deliberately, *hijo…* he perked up into his tiptoe dance, fidgeted with an invisible bowtie, and smooched and smooched. Salvadora didn't say anything else. She knew Henry was leaving Nicaragua to live with her sister. He had to.

Salvadora dressed Henry in immaculate shirts, white for his uniform and pale colors for when he was out of school, *lilac, yellow, celeste,* when Henry came into the house, she called for him to change

80

before he went back out, but she hadn't spoken her last word when Henry was already in the street *boleando*, scooping a ball (an old tube sock wrapped around a rock) off the wet cobblestone and flinging it to his neighbor, Teodoro, *un amigo*. Laughing ecstatic, Henry loved to play, like a cooped-up puppy, he waited feet wide and hands flowered out for the ball, tongue lapping his mouth, *jaja, toss it here, Teodoro, c'mon, toss it.* Henry chopped his feet as the ball came at him, erupting in cheers if he caught it and quickly slung it back; when he missed and had to chase the ball down the block *a la gran puta, Henry!* it didn't matter that the boys gave him grief *hurry, caballo.* It was still fun, *you suck, Henry, jodido,* running as hard and fast as he could. Salvadora came to the door with a wooden spoon in hand *Henry, hijo, come eat,* he hadn't eaten a thing since his breakfast and he sprinted to her, kissed and smothered her, near slobbered, but no, he wasn't hungry, he was going to go play with his friends at the park, *they're waiting, mama.* Later, he said with several pecks and a big suffocating hug. He'd eat. And with his favorites, *con maduros y crema y tiste.*

I made albondigas soup.

Sí, mama. Later. And don't forget. Con maduros y crema y tiste.

Sí, hijo, the food will be warm when you get home.

Salvadora smiled, *mañoso, peculiar.* Soup didn't go with plantains and sour cream. He liked what he liked.

Ideay, Henry, campeón, we're leaving, hombre, Teodoro whistled loud and impatient.

Henry held her hands, like sweethearts do, and told his

mother he had to leave, *los chavalos*, he said. *Sí, hijo. Your friends.*
She yelled at them to look out for her Henry*, you hear.*

Teodoro, take care of Henry, oíste. If you don't, I'll tell
your mother you're up to no good. Oíste.

Teodoro waved to Salvadora, assured her, *claro que sí.* His
mother would hear about it, she warned again, if anything went
wrong. Salvadora watched her boy run off, all windmill elbows and
heels kicking high into the air.

But *los chavalos eran bien jodidos.* They were bad.
Misbehaved. Looked for trouble. Hmm.

Everyone was fond of Henry in Barrio Monseño Lescano.
Loved him, *skinny fool.* They quickly started a baseball game.
Henry pounded the bat on the pavement, and *hueputa, dammit,
man*, the boys complained that he was chipping it, pitched the
ball hard on purpose so that Henry missed and corkscrewed out
of control, which was fun for him *calm your ass down* and he kept
spinning on purpose *dundo, you nut* as he handed the bat to the
next hitter. On defense, Henry wished for the ball, he was a riot,
clapped and clapped and yelled *here, right here.* The boys sent him
deep into the outfield, so far that his chatter was a murmur. But
he stayed ready. Shouted so they knew he was. The ball reached
him once, just once all game. *Cool, tuani.* Baseball was wonderful,
of course it was, Henry was Nicoya, *pinolero*, and he dreamt of
playing baseball, not professionally, not in las grandes ligas; just in
the street with his friends, every day after school.

The boys played until the long shadow of a battered
factory covered the lot they called a park, cooled everything, took

the life out of the game.

Ideay, Teodoro, what do you say, chele?

Duglas was an older boy, maybe twenty. He stood where brick walls had been knocked down and left a makeshift stage, the surviving A-N-T-A from a logo in the background. He stuck a cigarette in his mouth and patted his breast pocket, swept it with fingers. No lighter.

A la puta, don't got my lighter. Teodoro, don't you have a lighter to lend me, jodido?

No, hombre.

No shit. Matches?

Not even, Duglas.

No lighter, ni mierda, he was fucked, he mumbled.

Duglas looked around aimless, mimed striking a lighter in his hand. He wiggled his thumb high for everyone to see. The other boys looked at Duglas blankly.

Loan me a chelín. I can buy one at the store.

Teodoro pulled his pockets inside out, exaggerated.

Nada, broder. He was broke, *pero bien palmado*.

Not even a quarter! Hijueputa. No one has …?

The boys shook their heads dumbly, bit their lips.

Que barbaridad. You guys ain't worth shit.

They smiled sheepish, chuckled, *screw you*.

He needed a smoke, broder. It was bothering him. *Let's go to my tía's, chele*. Duglas' aunt lived close.

Dale pues.

A couple of boys followed Duglas and Teodoro across the

street to the tía's house. Mopeds and a small pickup beeped as they sped through them, *que es la verga*. The rest of the group kicked at stones on the ground and left for home.

Henry ... c'mon, man!

He scampered to catch up, froze a moment in the street as a couple on bicycle swerved to avoid him.

Duglas told everyone to wait outside as he slipped into a square pink house with a green door. Teodoro leaned against the fender of a rusty diesel truck, a boy hopped onto the empty flatbed. No one else was around except for an old man sitting in his doorway down the block, black frame glasses, loose tank top, a folded handkerchief in his hand for the heat as a transistor radio crackled between his feet. It was still stifling in the early evening. In the distance at the very end of the street, there was the lake and behind it the drove of calderas, Apoyeque and partners puffing gaseous vapor, and above them, Momotombo steamed, active, maybe today, *tal vez mañana*, at any moment the white plumes could become smoke and ash churning miles into the sky, the earth would buckle and throw tsunamis across Xolotlán, across Lake Managua, cover the people in mud, sludge, silt, preserve their final screams in mid-escape, mid-embrace like at Pompeii. When he was little, Henry asked his mother what was inside volcanoes, *nada, dirt, stones, heat*, and why were there so many like Santiago, Concepción, San Crístobal, *I don't know, hijo, Nicaragua is all cerros, así es*. Bisabuela Mercedes, Salvadora's grandmother, told her that Momotombo meant 'boiling top' in nahuatl, *what*, nahuatl was what the indios spoke, and they named him Momotombo, *we're all indios, hijo,* and then they were going to change his name, *who wanted to change his name – los españoles,* and Momotombo got mad, *se encachimbó,* and he shook and shot fire into the sky so they, *los españoles,* left him alone. He was proud of his nahuatl name, *like my name, Henry – sí, hijo.* Another time, she told him, long ago, Masaya, outside the colonial city of Granada, erupted and the people were afraid, a river of lava was threatening to destroy the city but a priest stood in front of it with a cross and Masaya stopped the molten flow. The city was saved, a miracle. But Henry didn't have to fear volcanoes. Because of them there was good land and all kinds of trees and plants and flowers and the cerros were full of animals, too, *monkeys – sí hijo, monkeys everywhere,* there were pacas, armadillos, tamanduas, spotted cats called tigrillos, pecarís, those were little hairy pigs, lizards all kinds, many birds like guardabarrancos, warblers, chachalacas, jays, macaws, parakeets, *we call them chocoyos,* hummingbirds, or colibrís. Bisabuela Mercedes adored colibrís, chirped at them and described each variety as it zipped into the yard, each one had a special flower that fit its beak exactly and it only sipped nectar from that particular flower; sapphire caps, ruby throats, emerald breasts, the *viejo caciques,* the old chiefs, wore the iridescent feathers in their capes, shimmery, glittery, fit for royalty, but hummingbirds were fierce, *pleitistas,* little fighters, they said a warrior that died in battle became a hummingbird, a *huitzilín,* to fly around forever from blossom to blossom, *runruneando, zumbando.* When she was very old, Bisabuela Mercedes sat for hours in the yard, hands folded, head tilted back, still, just her eyes tracking the little warriors that darted around her overgrown garden, they were her favorite things, her mouth hung open in delight as they flicked up and down, hovered over a new bush. That was how they found her one day, her eyes open as though she were still watching them flit about. Henry was Salvadora's huitzilín, strong, radiant, loved all things sweet.

Duglas came out sipping from a large fuchsia cup.

I'm thirsty, broder.

Teodoro motioned impatiently. Duglas handed him the cup. He took a gulp and coughed the drink out through his nose. Duglas cackled hysterically, took the cup back before Teodoro dropped it.

A la gran puta, jodido, what did you give me?

Guaro. My tía makes it.

Bruto, that shit burned my asshole, no jodas.

Duglas sipped more guaro and passed the cup to the other boys. Each took a trial taste then a drink, screwed their faces, hacked and laughed. Duglas could've at least offered 7-Up with it. *No jodas, mamón. Shut up and drink.* The boys were bolder the second round. They chatted animated meandering through topics, except for the obvious.

What's up with your girl, tu jaña?

Teodoro had a girlfriend, kinda sorta, he saw her on afternoons when he found himself sitting on a stool, chewing a stem lost in thought and then it occurred to him to grab his bicycle and go see her, Tula. He walked her to the market for fresh tortillas y chicharrón, and then they spoke through an open gate until dusk and it was time for Tula to go inside, a peck on his cheek, bye.

¿Did you screw her, chele?

Teodoro flicked a butt at Duglas, *shut up*, for being a jerk, *tapudo*, and asking the wrong shit. The boy on the flatbed yelled *ideay* for another drink and a cigarette, legs swinging content, he complained about the lighter and tapped it forcefully on the planks, ignored Duglas' empty threats of beatings and turcazos if he broke his tía's chispero. Duglas danced to a salsa in his head and the other boy, in a Hi-C t-shirt, commented that he must have ants up his butt, never in one spot, *super inquieto, el salvaje*, they laughed, drank, *no, seriously, broder, qué pasa, what's up with Tula.* Duglas leaned on him but Teodoro said nothing about Tula, stuck his nose in the fuchsia cup and swigged.

Ideay, loco, you're not drinking?

Duglas offered Henry guaro. He looked to Teodoro.

Don't be afraid, broder.

Henry waited for what to do.

Go ahead, don't be a dumbass. Mamón. Duglas held it closer.

Teodoro nodded, pointed at the cup with his puckered mouth. Henry took it with both hands and drank.

Este maje – this dude is headed north.

Everyone looked at Henry, *chocho, is it true, loco, you're going to the States,* Henry nodded as he tipped the cup back, nodded energetic as he pounded his chest, hacked hard, *careful, it's not pinolillo, Henry, caballo.* Teodoro patted his back, they chuckled as Henry held out the cup for whoever would take it first, a big caricature smile. Duglas grabbed his shoulder and shook him affectionately, *so then, you're leaving us, campeón,* a hanging horse smile, yes, Duglas sighed deep *chocho,* digested the news, shook Henry again, *bueno, take another drink, loco,* he wasn't going to find guaro in the states so *have another and good luck.* Teodoro told Duglas to take it easy, Henry didn't drink. *Tranquilo, broder,* Duglas wasn't going to harm Henry, they were celebrating, *a going away party,* the boy in the Hi-C t-shirt began to tell the story about a neighbor, Moises, it was yesterday, two soldiers came to his house and entered the door like they were in their own damn home, *bastards,* they were inside awhile, *a long while,* the front door was open but black like outer space, nothing was visible, until Moises finally emerged, two soldiers with their rifle butts in his back, he traipsed down the middle of the street, head slung low, not knowing where to put his hands and he was gone, *el broder.* They took him to the mountains to fight. Moises was never coming back. His parents were inside when they took him, but there wasn't any noise, no commotion, no one screamed or complained. Later, his mother, Doña Chelita was outside for a long time, arms crossed, after Moises had left. She hadn't watched him go. She just stared into a smelly mucky puddle along the curb. No one said anything to her, left her alone. *Say what, do what.* Moises was gone. The boys were quiet.

Bueno, Henry was leaving but it was good news. Duglas sipped and pressed the fuchsia cup against Henry's bony chest. *Drink, broder, the states don't know shit about guaro.* Chocho.

It was overcast, which made Managua tolerable, *fresco*. Washing clothes in the small yard, it was an innocuous afternoon, the same obligation, the same weariness. Salvadora scrubbed a powder blue shirt on the cement *lavadero*, pounded and wrung the water out then handed it to Henry to pin to the line.

What am I going to do at Tía Chayo's, mama?

Study. Meet your cousins, make friends. The sea is beautiful where she lives. You'll be happy, hijo.

I want to study here, mama.

You'll study over there, hijo. Find a job. A house. Una novia, maybe get married.

Novia, the idea embarrassed Henry, *him married*, he laughed, blushed at the silly suggestion, scratched his throat.

A no, mama.

Sí, one day you'll marry.

Henry looked at his mother, incredulous, mouth gaping. Salvadora raised her eyebrows and nodded insistently. He'd get married and she'd become a grandmother. God permitting.

Really, mama, me caso?

Sí.

No. Estás loca, mama.

Your mother isn't crazy. You're going to have a lovely life, Henry. Vas a ver.

Banging and a yell came from inside the house.

Pase!

La Daisy, who lived a few blocks away called out for Salvadora, who answered that she was outside, but Daisy didn't hear her and shouted back *where, I can't hear you,* so Salvadora stopped scrubbing and yelled over her shoulder into the house *the patio – adónde – el patio, hombre.* Finally, Daisy appeared in the backdoor *I couldn't hear* and sat on a stool next to the large tinaja of cool water. She wore a pink floral dress, her long brown hair in a simple bun. She was pretty, *linda.* Salvadora sent Henry to get Daisy a glass of *tiste,* it was all she had to offer. He went quickly then said he was going outside. But only out front, his mother warned. He wasn't going anywhere else*, oíste.*

Y ese milagro, how are you, Daisy?

More or less, mujer. And you, what's new? Henry was so grown, like his father, Daisy thought but made no mention.

These damn boys, they took Henry to play baseball but then got him drunk on *guaro,* and he came home a mess, giggling like a fool, her son didn't drink but his *supposed amigos* liked to mess with Henry, and he didn't know when they were teasing him. He just says he was with friends, mama. They were playing. She found him against the doorjamb, barely able to stand, alone, scoundrels didn't have the guts to stay with him until she answered the door. *Sinvergüenzas.*

Salvadora snapped a shirt and pinned it to the line. She noted how dark the sky was, maybe rain. Strange. Ojalá que no. She'd have to take down all the laundry. Salvadora slapped a sudsy shirt on the *lavadero* and scrubbed. *Puchica,* Henry ruined his clothes with his friends.

Daisy…

Salvadora looked up to find her friend holding the glass.

She hadn't taken a sip. Tears fell into her lap.

Daisy, what's wrong?

Jairo. They took him.

People had been talking about things getting worse, the fighting was escalating and soldiers were needed, so they talked, Daisy and her husband, their other two sons were too little, but Jairo was of age, so Sergio said it was best to take him out of Managua, far from here. They crossed the country to Bluefields where Sergio's family was. Jairo would be safe. But it turned out the fighting was building out there, too, in the swamp, in the middle of nowhere, *can you imagine, they take kids, the army came for kids*, they took Jairo to train him to fight, and Sergio was missing, too, well, he wasn't missing, he was arrested but his family didn't know anything about him *only that he was taken to jail* because he got in their way, he fought, he tried to keep Jairo from them, but no matter, they arrested him, which could mean he was dead. Jairo was just a boy, they say the whole army was just boys, *inocentes*, and even a few girls, Jairo didn't know how to fight, didn't know about the government, or the Sandinistas, *es solo un chavalo, just a boy*, they had him, *mi hijo, Salvadora, what do I do*, it'd been six weeks since he was taken. *Can you imagine, Salvadora*, how long it took for them to tell her Jairo was gone. What was she going to do. She had no idea where he was. How was that possible.

Salvadora was stunned. She dried her hands on a rag, faced Daisy, thinking what to say.

Lo siento, Daisy.

Daisy attempted to drink, then set the glass on the wide lip of the tinaja.

He was so happy to leave with his father. Jairo adored him. I thought, at least Jairo was going to be safe.

Salvadora knelt in front of Daisy, took her hands, kissed them. They cried together, shared few words the rest of that afternoon.

Henry was leaving as soon as Salvadora could make it happen.

Three months later, Daisy received word from a cousin of her husband that Jairo was wounded in a fire fight to take a hill outside Puerto Cabezas, he was shot through the leg and bled in the mud for hours before he was dragged out. He wasn't being moved. *What about Sergio?* The cousin didn't know. Assumed he was still under arrest. They both remained far away, in a part of the country almost foreign to people in the capital, a region unimaginable to a world that knew little to nothing of Nicaragua.

All the newcomers went to Mission High. Henry was happy to be in school. He was an eager student, bouncy, talkative, willing to share as much as he knew, chuckled at his mistakes, patient for corrections, and, at all times, respectful. He liked his teachers. He liked his classmates. He liked his lessons. School was where he wanted to be. Always. Tuesday after school, Henry went to his English class to write in his journal. Mr. Ross let him stay while he ran chess club, as long as he was quiet. Mr. Ross gave a stern look. And a wink. Henry laughed, *OK, profe. Mr. Ross*, the teacher corrected. *Sí, Mr. Ross.* Henry filled page after page of his composition notebook with brief descriptions of his favorite things, places, people, accompanied by squiggly but accurate doodles, his font and scrawling regular enough to be called a style, his artistic signature, his slant on life in panels. He delighted in his writings and illustrations, penciled carefully, tip of his tongue out, concentrated, worked every scribble until just right. Perfect. Henry held his notebook up to admire his work. He flashed that burlesque angular smile then moved on to the next panel. Mr. Ross noted Henry's joy, smiled light as he scrutinized the student moves on the chessboard, White's Queen to g4, Black's light-squared Knight to f6, White's Pawn to c4, Black's Queen to a5, White's Queen to g5, way too much use of the queen.

Henry, do you want to play? Mr. Ross waved him over.

Oh no, profe. No, gracias.

Are you sure? It can be fun.

No, gracias, Mr. Ross. I want to write.

Mr. Ross crossed his arms comfortable and wondered out loud about the endgame, what if there was no queen, what were the other pieces worth, what was your opponent thinking, what to do with no queen, was there a plan. What was the next best possible move.

It was an hour of thoughtful expression twice a week in Room 325.

The chess club meeting ended and the chess team exited. Mr. Ross checked in at the doorway and said he would see them all

Thursday. *Check you out, Mr. Ross.* Henry continued to work in his notebook. Mr. Ross stood at his elbow, observed. Henry pressed his pencil hard, gently brushed away graphite bits. Mr. Ross asked what he was drawing. It was the central park in Granada, where he went to visit his Tía Chabela, the branches of the mango trees hung low with ripe fruit, strained, but even then they were out of reach, so the children had to throw rocks or find branches that they stripped to make sticks long enough to poke the mangos free. That was him in the center of the park throwing rocks. Henry was terrible, he never knocked a mango loose. All his rocks disappeared into the thick foliage and clacked on the terracotta tile roof of a hotel, or fell on *gente*, folks promenading the colonial streets, *ay, Henry, careful*, and he'd go into his nervous apologetic dance *o lo siento*, he didn't mean any harm. Mr. Ross leaned over Henry, asked about the other people he drew, who were they; one was his friend, Teodoro, who he'd known since they were little from their barrio, Monseñor Lescano, he was nice, he liked *cajeta de frijol*, a candy made from bean paste; one was his primo Giovanni, who chewed on cigars because when he was a toddler he picked the whitewash off the walls in their house and ate it freely until it made him sick, he vomited and shook and cried frustrated but as soon as he calmed, hands soothing his gross belly, Giovanni ate some more, so Tía Chabela, *his mama*, gave Giovanni cigars to chew instead. He was crazy. The rest were just boys and girls, *los chavalos de aquí y allá, who hang out in the park, in the barrio.* Mr. Ross inspected the figures, read the descriptions. He turned the pages, said the journal was becoming a marvelous history. Henry liked to explain his work. Traced the figures as he recounted a time that she… or the one time when he… Henry touched each word as he read his text. Twice a week, that was how he spent his afternoon.

I didn't drive. My friends from high school — I went to a private school outside the barrio — all got their driver's licenses as soon as they were 16, drove an old family car, made quick money for a used car, or killed themselves to get their dream car, a Chevelle, a GTO, an Impala. My homeboys from the neighborhood didn't drive; they stayed on the block, kicked back with 40s and a suitcase-sized boom box, had a cousin who drove when they needed a ride, but otherwise, they walked to the house party cuz it was just right over there, right next to John O'Connell High, across from El Faro Taquería at Maricela's mother's house, *you know her, right, curly hair, kinda thick*. I didn't give a fuck about cars. I saw it as money I didn't have, but more it was just I didn't care. No god damn interest in getting my dream ride. My stepfather loved his fucking cars, bought one then moved on to another one, and another one, in his mind each time more stylish, classy, he spent his money easy, added spoilers and rims, seat covers, chrome details, and kits. He never treated mama so good, and I saw that. It stayed with me. He took better care of his car than her. After their break up, he still came around the house to keep tires and fenders and brake parts in her garage. *We're only separated*, mama said, *giving ourselves some space* until mama finally had enough of his bullshit fuckery behind her back and in her face, and she took a claw hammer to his goddamn windows one night. So, motherfuck cars, for real. I walked to my friends' houses if I wanted to hang out. If there was a party somewhere far, I got rides with homeboys. They bitched about it, gave me hella shit the whole ride over, but whatever, they were my homeboys. I never learned to drive, and I still didn't. I walked like always. Everywhere. And I rode the bus.

It was sunny and hot and I was riding the 14 Mission. I read a magazine in my lap, swayed and jerked as the bus managed traffic. It was early afternoon. A shitty time to drive in the Mission. I wiped sweat into my temple. Windows were open but it didn't help. The bus lurched, stopped, hissed. Someone bounded past and plopped hard into a seat across from me. I recognized him immediately, taller, muscled in the shoulders but lanky, strong jaw, and a wispy mustache. A man but same comical smile. Unforgettable.

He rode staring out the window, mouth moving in whispers, reminders. I played it off like I wasn't watching him. It was a trip how you just saw people. Folks from a long ass time ago, showing up, random. Forever in the neighborhood. I didn't think he recognized me. If he did, he wasn't trippin. Why would he be.

The Boys' Club drew dudes from 20th Street to the Valencia Gardens projects to the Harrison railroad tracks, and it was cold-blooded, fuckin unkind, and dudes had to be ready to snap, handle themselves, cuz fuckheads was always cappin, shit talkin and starting static every fucking minute of every fucking day. If your name was Roshawn then you were Roach, if your pants had hella stains then you were Dirty, if you had a low thick ass brow then you were Caveman; there was Wolfman cuz of his wavy ass hair, Baby Huey cuz he was big as fuck and doughy, Froggy from Our Gang cuz he was a white boy in the projects and fuckin looked like that kid, Barracuda cuz of his big ass gapped teeth, and this one dude wore a white sweatshirt over a white Polo shirt with white jeans and Adidas Attitudes without thinking about it, so then he was Milkman, not for the rest of middle school but the rest of his fucking life. Always cappin. We got on each other's mama until we couldn't take anymore and broke, or we fought, *be talkin too much, man, watch*. It was also dap, *what's up witchu*, check out a foosball and let's get a game going. Me and Jeek are playin, *too late, blood*, call winners, don't be cheatin, dude, I wish you would, *lemme get a quarter*, trippin; copper tooling in the crafts shop over the PA speaker; who got winners, *you do after Seb and Droopy*, Marlon shooting from goalie through everybody's men, dudes frozen, *he don't look it but he's bad*; biddy basketball, dogcatcher on the PA speaker; *for real lemme get a quarter*, trippin, we gonna be here all day, blood, tellin you. Why, cuz you got Marlon, *bang* damn straight, you ain't about shit though, your mama still love me, *who got winners*, talkin all that smack. *Let's split a bag of chips then*, a Coke, hot dog, Now-or-Laters, *I want some, too*, trippin. *Bang*, game point. *Marlon doin'all the work, you talkin all that smack*, Lemonheads, popcorn, a 7-Up, just a zip, don't backwash, blood. *Bang*, that's game. *Just cuz you got Marlon*. Trippin. That was the forever chatter of the games room, it always ended with let's get another game then, one more game, a challenge to give a dude a chance to get you back, be cool, don't be like that, one more.

Better call winners then, and wait your turn, weak blood. Shit.

There was space for quiet dudes, too, like the ceramic studio, glazing sculptures cut and scored from a single clay tile; the wood shop showed dudes how to sand and varnish a simple set of drawers for 35¢; maybe learn to print black and white photos in a dark room, silk screens in the art room, or lounge with D&D, graphic novels and board games in the library. These were dudes with for real hobbies, who pursued enthusiasms, and spent hours gabbing about spells, J. R. R. Tolkien, hobbits, balrogs, the Silmarillion, Coeurl, the Cthulhu Mythos, Elric of Melniboné, races of orcs, the vorpal sword and wall of blades and how that came from the bible, *forget you, the Bible*, they were talking about fantasy and magic and folklore, pure make-believe, supernatural and shit, storytelling, *the bible, hah, how you figure*, they were talking about wizards and goblins. *Dude, the flaming sword was at the gates of Eden*, and spirits, like the Valar and Maiar, right, fought evil like archangels, like in the bible. *Forget you, man. The bible ain't sci-fi.* These dudes knew how to have conversations and shit. They discussed topics, right. Gentle souls. Thoughtful. Goofy asses but nice.

There was space, too, for boys coming to the club for the first time, who were new to everything. Boys from Nicaragua and El Salvador, their families fleeing war, clean short hair, formal leather shoes, uncool like passport photos, they surged through the club in electric masses, rabbles, they were loud and squawked *cerotes* and *hijueputas* and *a la vergas*, howls, cackles, they filled the lobby, swarmed hallways and staircases horse playing, clapped each other on the back, pulled ears, *que jodas vos*, unruly, noisy like a chicken coop until the club director had to break them up, *boys,* shouted over them, and they chuckled, elbowed ribs like they were all in on it, a big fucking joke on the director, who didn't speak the language, *boys*, inside, *boys*, gag funnier because he didn't understand, *que es la verga, hombre*, but the director did the best he could, separated them, *por favor amigos*, pick a place, they needed to be in an area, billiards, scooter football, woodcut prints. Any place but the staircase, the hallway, or the lobby. They needed to find a spot to be. And stay. Henry was with them, gaping mouth smile, gangly, black mop of hair. He needed to find a place, too.

I spent a lot of time in the gym, playing ball and talking shit. Henry burst in one day, long thin legs poking out of over-sized green shorts like they wore in the Army, skipping in dress shoes and circling the basketball court like an animal let out of a pen.

It was whiffle baseball season, and the gym was full. The batting team sat on the floor along first base, and dudes who wanted to watch bunched together against the outfield wall. We took the game super serious. We played to win. Hated losing. We wanted our names on a copper plate added to the champions plaque. It was baseball with a stupid plastic ball, but it was still winning. Games mattered.

We were up, Eduardo led off. As soon as someone picked up the bat, the chatter started, look at his legs, look at his ears, look at his stomach, look at his lips, look at his butt, shorts all up his ass and shit, he's too white, he's too ashy, he's too skinny, he's fat as fuck, his shirt is faded, he's got crust on his neck, he's got wax in his ears, he's nappy, his shorts are hella tight, hella high, baggy, you can see his drawers, you can see his butt crack, you can see his nuts, he's got on whackers, he's got a hole in his shoe, you can see that fool's dirty socks and his belly and his nalgas and his huevos.

Eduardo made a quick out. Henry was up. We picked our own teams for the league but the gym director added random dudes that wanted to play. Henry was our random dude. He pounded home plate with the plastic bat and dudes started to bust up. He grinned wide as he stood straight up in his black leather shoes and waited for the ball. Henry swung fiercely at the first pitch and sprinted to first base, shrieking and squealing and howling the whole way, jubilant, clamorous all by himself. He was safe at first, happy. He clapped hard, cheered *vamos*. The gym erupted. Dudes fell over themselves, rolled and yanked at each other's shirts talking about *he was hella screaming, dude thought he won the world series, he was like bwahhh, he sounded like a fire engine, running for his life and shit.* Henry kept clapping until the next kid hit the ball. After that, we all waited to see if he'd do it again. And he did. That was how he played baseball.

Late in the game, the score was tied. There was a runner on second and Henry was up. He swung and went howling up the line like before. It was a foul. We giggled as he walked back to home.

Carlos met him with the bat in his hand.

What're you doin? Quit fuckin around! We need a fuckin hit!

It got quiet, still. Henry looked confused, his grin was awkward, ill, he looked to us, let out a nervous laugh.

Shut up! It echoed. The fuck you laughin about?

Carlos was a big dude, pot-bellied but he had brawny shoulders and chest. He held the bat like he was about to hit Henry. We stared, our eyes big and dry. Henry closed his mouth, cowered. He felt his waist for pockets.

Fuckin be ready. We need a hit.

Carlos stuck the bat in Henry's chest, thumped him.

Henry walked to the plate. He waited patiently, bat resting on his shoulder. Carlos cheered him on, *c'mon blood, let's go*, booming claps, he coached him in Spanish, *tocala a tercera, let's go, let's go*. No one else made any kind of noise. Henry swung and stung a line drive into the corner. He made it to second and we scored. Carlos roared, *fuck yeah, blood*, he clapped his hands raw and pumped a fist at Henry, who looked over and managed a meek smile, suppressed a quiver. He watched for the next pitch, hands on knees as Carlos cheered on. *Like I fuckin told you, blood.*

Henry had one more at bat. He swung hard and hit a weak flyball to center. Then he laid the bat down and walked out of the gym. A brisk, steady sulk from home plate through the panic doors in centerfield. I never saw him again. At the club. Or anywhere.

Everyone looked miserable, beaded with sweat. The bus labored on Mission. Henry looked out the window with dreamy eyes, head swaying on his neck like a long palm. Two women romped to the back and took empty seats behind and in front of Henry. They were older homegirls, tough, tank tops and jeans. The white woman wore a thick, studded leather bracelet and letters tattooed on her fingers. Her dirty blonde hair was feathered. She faced Henry, looked him up and down. The other homegirl was Native. Her long black hair spilled all over her shoulders, lustrous and elegant like a cape. She smiled ear to ear. A crucifix was inked between her thumb and index finger. The white woman leaned close to Henry.

You're cute. Her voice was husky, gravelly.

Henry snapped out of his dreaming and looked at the woman. Her smile was crooked, eager. Henry smiled back, fiddled with his collar.

Ooo…you are cute. Isn't he cute, Ramona?

Yeah. Ramona's grin was hyena. She scratched a boob. Yeah.

Henry grinned at Ramona but all shy. He massaged his neck.

What's your name, love? The white woman tapped his knee.

Henry.

You got a girlfriend, huh? Just say no.

No. He giggled, not able to answer anything else.

Henry, you wanna come with us? I'm Sally. That's Ramona. You wanna come with us, Henry?

Oh, Henry. Yeah. Ramona nodded, scratched her chest. Yeah.

I have work. Henry sat up. I work.

You got a job, love… Hear that, Ramona?

Yeah. She sunk into her seat, knees wide apart. Henry gets better all the time, man.

Henry swiveled between Ramona and Sally. He checked the windows, looked to the front of the bus. Sally passed Ramona a bottle of iced tea. She chugged it noisily, offered Henry a swig. It was hot as hell outside. A nice day to hang out.

Henry told his mother he saw la Cegua, from the legend, the witch, who was a pretty girl but turns ugly, real ugly, mama. She was nice to him, she was pretty, *no era mala*, she didn't punish Henry for being bad, like she did to the *mujeriegos, borrachos*, out all-night womanizing and drinking, who lost their minds after seeing a horse's face expecting to kiss a beautiful girl; no, she wasn't like the legend, mama. Her dress was white and made of *garuma* leaves. Her hair hung to her waist in twists of cabuya like twine and it danced as she spoke. *Estás loco vos, that's the legend. No, mama, she was nice.* The men called her la Cegua because they were all in love with her, they filled her ears with promises, and fairy tales, their insufferable begging and garbled pleas, the babbling of crazed idiots, *babosadas, foolishness, bullshit,* their nonsense was enough to drive her insane, it was tiring, boring, better they spent those words on their *mujeres*, whoever waited for them at home. All that mattered was whether they had enough pesos. *If not, leave her the fuck alone. Puchica.*

Teodoro and Duglas had asked Henry if he wanted a girlfriend, *I don't have a girlfriend – exactly*, they knew a girl who would be his girlfriend, she was beautiful, simpática, guapa, he was going to like her, *really*, all he had to do was ask her out, *no fooling*, take her to eat, *the closest open grill, fritanga,* buy her carne asada y tostones, tell her how pretty she was and she'd be your girlfriend, *really*. They were stinking drunk when they showed up at her house. Duglas disappeared immediately to look for more *guaro* and left Teodoro to talk to la Cegua, how was she, how had she been, he had a friend he wanted her to meet, *a la gran puta, you're both drunk, man, you stink*, no, no, Henry was alright, *he's a good dude,* gentle, *educado*, a sweetheart, she was going to like him. He thrust Henry to her, *soy Henry, will you be my girlfriend?* La Cegua couldn't help herself, smiled. Henry stumbled forward and she caught him under the arms, *Henry, estás mal*, he explained that he wasn't *mal*, he was fine, content, he was with his friends, they played baseball, they listened to the radio and told *chiles, jokes,* he drank a little *guaro*, a little; she was pretty, *muy bonita* like his mother, who had dark eyes like tamarind, *the seeds*, they shined, like the black rocks along the highways, there were fields of black stones, everywhere, broken into smaller pieces and inside, inside was where they were shiny, like mama's eyes, she was pretty just like his mama, *gracias*, shiny like her, *shined like little pretty stones*. La Cegua said the stones came from volcanoes, *I know like Momotombo, Azul,* yes, Henry, *Cegua, be my novia – my name is Monserrat,* was that like a volcano name, she didn't know, maybe it was, did she still want to be his girlfriend, *sí, Henry*, she held him, steady with her hand between his shoulder blades, *you're so drunk, Henry, estás mal*. He mumbled into her shoulder, neck and she said to stop, *hush*, it tickled her, Henry pulled on her sleeves to keep himself up, fingers dug into her dress. Suddenly, he was lead, dead weight. Monserrat called for her Tío Pichito. She dropped Henry into his oxcart, and *el tapudo de Teodoro, too*, who was head between knees asleep on her doorstep. Pichito drove them both home, the wooden wheels making an infernal racket in the quiet night.

Henry told his mother that la Cegua agreed to be his girlfriend, she was pretty like her, same black obsidian eyes, *what're you talking about*, Salvadora told him to shut up as she undressed him and put him to bed. *Estás loco vos.*

Sally played with Henry's hair, swept his bangs. Henry smiled, and shriveled a bit but let her. Henry didn't know what else to do. Ramona laughed loud, lively.

Fucking cute and shit. She scratched her boob again.

What time do you get out of work, love? We'll go by and see you. We'll go out. It's a beautiful day. It'll be nice.

Yeah. We'll get you high, babe. Yeah.

Sally put her hand on Henry's knee, walked her fingers up his leg. He giggled, clutched his collar. She tickled him under his chin. He couldn't stand it but did his best not to lose it on the bus.

What do you say, Henry? Come with us. Get high.

Suddenly, the bus braked and threw everyone forward. Holy shit. Fuck. God damn. Objects slid across the floor. The crowd groaned, wondered what the fuck was going on. A few folks complained about being late, goddamn bus needed to get moving, for real. It felt like it was forever. Outside, there were police officers and lookie-loos clustered in the intersection. It was several more minutes of squirming in slick plastic seats and mumbling for a place to set groceries, but eventually, the news made it to the back of the bus.

The driver had hit an old lady. Passengers stood up to see. Nothing. Folks started asking if anyone had heard anything. Nothing. We didn't hear anything at all before it happened. The driver never even honked the horn.

18.

My lady liked the way the quesadillas were grilled at La Taquería. Otherwise, I would never go there. I did go when I was young, when it was just another taquería in the Mission, faceless, unremarkable among the dozens others and the last one to come across, just ordinary and way the hell out of the way on 25th Street, it was well before the hysteria and amusement park lines. Walking in and about the neighborhood, *vago* that I was, I can't recall what brought me that far up Mission from 19th, maybe walking to the arcade on 30th, maybe walking to Upper Noe Park, or top of the hill Daly City for the hell of it on an empty afternoon. I must've been hungry, duh. I must've wanted a burrito, not tacos. I just happened to be on 25th. But I went in no more than two or three times. The lady that took the orders was a dick, pushed you along, gave a mean, sore look if you took a moment to think, talked to you — at least to me — like her time was being wasted, irritated. She never looked at you. And then charged a dollar extra for crema, a dollar extra for aguacate, a dollar extra for salsa. Fuck. That lady and the prices were reason enough to go somewhere else.

It was 1987 when La Taquería was just another taquería. Now it was a zoo.

The lady was still here. She still had that look like she smells something foul, but not for the white folks. Never for the white clients. She'd have to be out of her mind. On the contrary. Maybe even a smile for the gringos. No matter. I wasn't in her line.

I ordered in that informal manner, in a way rude, talked into space as I read the menu, assumed someone was listening, not caring enough about the person to look into her eyes.

Una quesadilla suiza, super, no crema.

Algo más?

Solamente.

Then it crossed my mind I was going to be waiting for a while.

Sabe que — una cerveza, por favor. Dos Equis.

Maestrooo…

I looked up, startled. The woman taking my order scrutinized me, eyebrows raised. I was at a loss for words, embarrassed like I was caught being bad. Shit. I've done worse. Stumbling drunk in the streets. Fumbling with keys in the dark. Cussing loud enough for the neighbors to hear.

Está bien, maestro. Es viernes.

I relaxed, gave a meek smile. Yes, it was fine. It was Friday evening.

A beer does no harm. But just one, maestro.

She held up one castigating finger and smiled, teasing. I acquiesced, crossed my heart. One, I said.

Don't be ashamed, maestro. How are you?

I was fine. I hadn't remembered yet who she was, but it had to be a parent that knew me from work.

Do you have plans for the weekend, besides the beer?

Watch a movie. Have another beer if I'm given permission.

Claro que sí, maestro. You deserve it.

She turned to get the beer from the refrigerator. I chuckled, patted my chest. She fucking got me. *Jodida*. When she came back with the bottle, I recognized her. Her daughter was in my ELD class. 2nd grade. Good kid. Liked to talk English. Liked to read a lot. She wanted to know more about the Japanese. Super into them. Said she wanted to be Japanese. Not like the Japanese, but a Japanese. Nice kid. Bright, like the nuns used to say to me.

Lo destapo?

Por favor.

She uncapped and slid the sweaty beer across the counter along with change.

Gracias.

Que le vaya bien, maestrooo...

I took a long pull and sidled into the crowd as openings appeared. It was shoulder to shoulder, full of chatter, boisterous, no one too concerned with the numbered tickets in their hands.

19.

A dozen or so men are lined up along a cinder block wall like prisoners awaiting execution by firing squad. Sharing their last smokes. Tightening the plastic tarps over cluttered shopping carts. Arms crossed. Bracing themselves against the cold. Or hugging themselves for warmth. They are the enemy, or perhaps deserters, in either case they deserve it.

They sit along the base, no other recourse but to give in, wait their fate. A hand on their cart so no one can walk away with their belongings if sleep happens to catch them unaware, slipping. Some of them are in full despair, hands in lap or arms hung over knees, head drooped acquiescent to the ax. It's cold. It's getting dark.

Mostly, they have no choice; wait until the shelter opens its doors and lets men in until capacity, and then it's the long night's march for a doorway for those who don't make it inside.

When I was little, the other side of this cinder block was my preschool. I spent tireless hours on heavy red tricycles in the spacious yard. I leaned into the pedals, rose off the seat to put my meager weight into the tricycle until the big solid wheel slowly began moving. I rode around in one direction, close to the walls, turning sharply at the corners. Once, I turned too late. The handlebar stuck into the wall and pinched my little finger. The mortar was jagged, squeezed out between the cinder blocks like icing. It scratched my hand badly. I had to drop off the seat and pull the tricycle back to free myself. My fingertip pulsed, turned dark purple. A couple of weeks later, the nail fell off.

The men who make it into the shelter will be safe for the night. They will get something to eat. They will sit on their cots and take deep breaths. Some will sleep. A few may have to leave. Some will worry about their things, who is going to watch their things while they sleep. In any case, it's better than being outside. It's better inside.

20.

Our regular perch was at the top of the structures. Squared pieces of timber shot up from the middle of the playground like a fairy tale castle surrounded by a sand mote. Nothing magical, enchanting and shit. Some rough beams bolted together. A creaky walking bridge suspended across cheap lattice towers. We were alone at the top. Free to smoke cigarettes. Say what we wanted. *Hey, is it true…* or *Dude, don't tell nobody…* It was away enough. We saw everything. The backyards behind the swings. Someone kept rabbits in outdoor cages. Another stacked beehives. The games on the cement baseball field. Three flies up. Baserunners. Dueling with folks that wanted to play soccer. In one direction was 19th Street. The other way were magnolias bunched in a corner near Valencia. Above, direct lines inside windows. There were dozens of windows. All sizes. Books on a shelf. Cans, jars of manteca, spices lined up above a stove. An empty shower curtain rod. We saw everything. We saw and watched everyone coming through. The playground was a thoroughfare. A rest stop. There was no magic, but it could be quiet, still.

It was late afternoon, long shadows striped the sand. The swings squeaked lightly when the wind blew. One swing seat thrown over the crossbar out of reach. A large pit left in the sand that reached the plastic sheets and gravel foundation. Bees buried inside jars. Food wrappers strewn on the slide. Empty bottles balanced, artfully, on beams. Most everybody was through playing and hanging out, and gone. Done.

Hardly anybody was left. Me and Eusebio were kicking back on the bridge. Annette and Rebecca were down in a corner scratching in the sand with sticks. I tossed a pebble at them but they didn't notice. I tossed a pebble closer. Annette raised a middle finger without looking up. She rested an elbow on Rebecca's knee as she reached with her stick. They giggled, talked quietly as they drew circles and wavy lines, a smiley face, scribbled hastily to start over. They shared gum, snapped it like fireworks. Annette dropped her stick abruptly and started to braid Rebecca's hair, but Rebecca waved her hands no, swatted mild to leave her hair alone. Annette pinched her shoulder after being rejected. Rebecca continued with a squiggly design. Annette bounced her knee, *inquieta*. Finally, she tugged on Rebecca's jacket and they got up, smoothed their clothes and walked carefully across the sand like they might trip. They headed out the back way. Towards Valencia. I tossed a pebble at them.

Hey, where're you guys going?

They looked back and smiled at us. I tossed another pebble, gave a playful sneer. Annette stuck out her tongue, flicked me off.

Store. Dork.

Annette, get me a Coke.

How about a Rojita?

Ha, we ain't in Managua. C'mon, get me a Coke.

You got money, Tonio?

No.

How about you, lumpy? You got any money?

Eusebio was caught off guard, put his hand to his chest like *who me*. He was just minding his own business. Rebecca waited for an answer hands on her hips like a school teacher. Eusebio gave her pleading hands, *pretty please*. Rebecca picked up one of my pebbles and threw it at us. Hard. We had to duck. She frowned and mocked Eusebio, pled with her middle fingers out. I rolled up a gum wrapper I found in my pocket and tossed it at them.

Don't be like that, Annette. Get me a coke. Please.

Rebecca nodded. Annette gave the ok sign, sarcastic.

For reals. Please, one Coke for both of us.

I waved, a formal kindly gesture. They waved back, brief, without looking, and continued out arm in arm.

You think they're coming back?

Naw, man, Seb. They ain't coming back. Just to bring your goofy ass a Coke? Hell naw.

I laughed about how they gave us the finger. Those girls were tough.

So, then it was just me and Seb hanging out, chatting. Mostly he was chatting.

You ever listened to The Clash?

Who?

The Clash.

Hell no, I've never listened to The Clash.

Well, it's this band…

Eusebio was a sponge, he soaked up everything his siblings had to say, his brother Mark, who enlisted in the Army and boxed in the service and wore his dog tags proud, cuz he accomplished something, cuz he cut it, basic training, four years of service, racist fucks from all across the country, proud cuz they didn't break him, he was a fit soldier and still a homeboy from fucking SF, a Mission head and what, and if it wasn't a story Mark told him, then it was his sister Esther handing down notes taken in requisite history classes at City College, like it was Seb getting his AA, too and shit, US Civics 1, Anthropology 2, English 1A and 1B, Calculus, he talked a lot about what it took to get a college degree, hundreds of pages to read each week and then come up with an original idea for a paper, Seb was like, for real, what's left to be said about Shakespeare, *Hamlet is about how revenge shows what it means to be human, right, but the real shit is Macbeth*, and then it was Evelyn and the latest movie she saw at either the Grande or the New Mission or a theatre downtown, like maybe the Regency, the St. Francis, or the big ass screen at the Coronet, *Apocalypse Now*, *The Wanderers*, *Alien*, *Rumble Fish*, *The Jerk*, *Videodrome*, *The Thing*, *Life of Brian*, Eusebio was up on every cool movie we needed to see, and he broke each one down for us in detail, giving us reasons to go check it out, what did we think, *we should go, right, right,* Eusebio chattered along until his sister Concha came to get him cuz what the fuck was he doing, it was hella late, their mom was calling, and he knew how much Concha hated to hear their mother screech into the alley like it could possibly reach the playground, it was time to go, stupid, before their mother got hoarse. Eusebio had 6 brothers and sisters, each of them towering, tall, man, his sisters, too, who were as tall if not taller than his brothers. He said their family was from a part of Mexico where the people were typically tall, Jalisco or something, and not just because of the Spanish but the indios from the area were hella tall, too. Mark, Concha, Esther and them deeply influenced Seb's interests, and he was committed to them. Especially the music, whatever turned them on, turned him out. Pink Floyd, Rush, Led Zeppelin, Patti Smith, The Ramones, Fuckin Allman Brothers, Queen, Fleetwood Mac, The Clash.

I had zero fucking idea about any of those bands. It wasn't soul/R&B. Not funk. Not salsa, no merengue. It didn't play on KDIA, KSOL or on anybody's boom box at the park. I had no cultural reference, *not hearing it, blood.* And it was nothing, I mean fucking nothing I expected from a Mexican kid in the barrio. Fuckin trip.

...Most of those bands were hella informed by blues music. They studied it like it was fuckin biology and shit. They knew about the blues from the beginning, man, how it came from whatchucallit spirituals that slaves sang in fields, and church music. They knew about the pioneers like Robert Johnson and what's his name — Leadbelly. Dudes were students, man. And they could play blues for real, like played it like they lived the blues, hurt and crying cuz they lost their old lady and had no money, came up picking crops and shit, or whatever; it was blues even though they were white boys, some from fuckin England. And these were rock bands. But you can hear it, the blues, in their guitar. It's a trip.

Fuckin dudes from England playing blues.

Hell yeah, they love American music. Especially Black music.

No shit.

A car revved loudly and roared up 19th. We both leaned back to see. It was a metallic red Impala with spoked rims. White hard top. We didn't know who it was.

…Lots of these dudes knew each other from playing clubs around where they lived and shit…

Where's that, Seb?

What?

Where they lived?

England.

Yeah, but where in England?

I don't know. London, Camelot, fucking Sherwood Forrest. Fuck if I know. The point is these dudes where running in the same circles, playing the same clubs, which was good because even though they had their own groups and making music and shit, they were figuring things out, right, so they went to shows and watched each other, and were like, holy shit, that dude's bad ass, right, fucking *this shit is new*, they pushed each other, then like they all broke up their bands and shit because they couldn't get along or were partying too much and fucking up, whatever, but they all wanted to keep playing and doing gigs…

What…?

Gigs, man.

What the fuck are those?

Shows, Tonio, they were fucking musicians and wanted to keep playing shows.

Oh. I got it. Go on…

Eusebio explained that they were all part of this inner circle, right, and talked to each other and shit, listened to music, fooled around with licks on their own and wrote down a few notes until some of them were like, hey, man, let's form a new band, what the fuck, they weren't doin shit all by their fuckin lonesome, right, and then that was how The Clash and Led Zeppelin got started. By fucking accident and shit. It was a trip, he said, how bands that bad ass, that influential that went on to change the world, barely got made.

How do you know so much about these bands? Who listens to — what's that — Led Zeppelin?

My brother Mark and sister Esther have all their albums. They listened to them when they started high school.

And now you listen to them?

Yeah, well, it's not like I have a fucking choice.

It was whatever they, his siblings, played in the house. His brother Mark told him about whatever he read in Rolling Stone. He read music magazines all day long and fell asleep with them on his chest.

And you ask him what he's reading?

Aw fuck naw, Eusebio didn't have to ask and couldn't avoid it if he wanted. Mark talked to him about articles in magazines while he was still reading them. He read the most interesting parts out loud. Eusebio would be taking a shower, and Mark would walk in and shit and started telling him how Black Sabbath wrote a lot of lyrics inspired by horror, or something or other.

But you don't mind.

It's cool. We talk a lot.

Just then some strange dude walked into the park. He wore a thick grey hooded sweater with a devil character drawn on the chest. Cholo style. He knew we were watching him but he didn't trip. He kept his eyes forward, hit a cigarette discreetly like a spy. He wasn't doing anything. He walked on past us with his hands deep in his front pouch.

You know him?

Nope, Seb, never seen him.

Dude walked on to the end of the rec building then somebody jumped out from behind the corner, all hugging and mobbing him. He squatted, put his thumbs in his ears and yelled boo. Dude in the hood made like he was going to punch him. Then they shook hands like homeboys and walked off leaning against each other, the new dude explaining something all excited to the dude in the devil hood, a finger in his chest the whole time.

So, what happened with these new bands?

Eusebio swallowed and thought a moment before he continued. These bands started out hungry, you know. They needed to play. Not like because they were artists and the music was their fuckin life but they were broke. They didn't have food. The lights were out. They needed to play so they could fill their stomachs. They weren't going to survive. They couldn't think about anything except the growling in their fuckin pansas, man. They had to be good, great. Later, when the bands were famous, then they could speak their minds about important shit.

Didn't they always have that choice? They could speak

their minds whenever they wanted. They wrote the songs.

Eusebio nodded in agreement. Yeah, but they weren't free to say whatever they wanted like make social commentary and be critical of the government, right, even though it was the right political climate, war, student demonstrations, riots, they had to wait until they had money, until they were rich and didn't have to worry about paying bills and shit. They could turn out to be terrible, they could suck and their band was done the next day. They never knew if and when they'd make it. They just had to go with their guts. Said fuck it and played their brand of music and shit. And if you didn't give a fuck about what anybody thought, then you were punk and shit.

Shoot. That's everybody then, blood.

What do you mean, Tonio?

That was everybody. All of us. This barrio, bro. Everybody around here was living and thinking about their stomachs. Man, they came from that shit. Folks came from countries where it had been lifetimes of empty bellies. Fucking biblical daily bread because all many people had was prayer. Corrupt governments after dictatorships. Abject poverty. No future. Our folks came here and it was still a monumental struggle. Maybe all they got was rice and beans. Meat was expensive. Just eating hella chicken and liver. Those big ass bricks of cheese people waited in line for at St. Charles Hall. Man, they worked minimum wage, broke their backs for a check and walked home consumed about whether there was going to be enough food. Plus clothes, rent, the lights, the heat, the laundry, gas, the phone, water, garbage, bus fare, the dentist, shots, medicine, birthdays, communions. Doing whatever else. Collected food stamps from Mi Rancho. Put things on layaway. Pawned meager gold chains and rings, hoped that one day they'd buy them back. *Just temporary.* They did whatever they needed to stay off welfare. My mother was punk rock as fuck then, working 16-hour days. Shit.

Fuck yeah, she is, dude.

Seb gave the rock on sign to the elements.

Eusebio, check it out.

From the structures, we saw into Ethan's modern flat. It had two square bay windows that led into the living and dining rooms. Ethan was home. He flashed back and forth, making the curtains sway. He slipped into the kitchen and then came right back out, his mother on his heels. Ethan called his mother Val, which we all thought was odd as hell. It wasn't right to call your mother by her first name. I could never ever imagine calling mama Dora Luz, like we were friends, not even good friends, like we just went to school together and happened to be in the same Algebra class. Be home and I'd be like, *Hey, Dora Luz, how are you? What's in the pan, gallo pinto? OK.* No fucking way. That was strange. How you gonna call your mother by her first name.

Ethan backed into the living room. His mother stood in the dining room, a hand on a chair. She was furious, shook the chair around. She ripped the glasses from her face and flung them aside. A fist on her hip. Ethan shouted at her. Loud. Foot-stomping screams.

It was like watching a movie.

Ethan continued to shout. Then Val moved closer to him. She kicked off her shoes. He yelled at her to leave him alone. He erupted and beat his chest. Val shouted back. Ethan stamped his feet. Then Val picked a wineglass off the table and threw it at him. It missed, shattered somewhere out of sight. She rushed him. Ethan raised his hands and covered up as Val pounced on him. He was a big kid, nearly as tall as his mother, a thick back, heavyset limbs, but he was an easy target, elbows to ears, cowering. She pounded on Ethan several times, swung straight down onto his back, savage, unrestrained, and then out of nowhere, she was swinging at him with a hairbrush and he fell to all fours, still elbows to ears, cowering.

Holy shit!

Fuck, dude!

We covered our mouths. Straightened up to get a better look.

Val beat Ethan's back until he disappeared behind a couch. She swung relentlessly. Several moments passed. Ethan never got up.

You see that?

Val stopped swinging and straightened up. She hurled the wide brush and stood for a while, her chest heaving. She ran her hands through her cropped hair, gripped it and smoothed it back before stepping over Ethan, and disappeared to the back of the flat into her bedroom.

Holy fuck, dude.

One time, I was at the corner store, Granada's, and Ethan's mother showed up. She didn't come inside, she stayed in the doorway. A bunch of us were crowded around a kid playing Defender, and she just started yelling at us. We didn't pay any mind at first, but then she began to escalate until one by one we turned around to face her, the shouting compelled us, telling us to leave her son alone, that she was going to fucking kill us if we didn't stop messing with Ethan. Val was sweating and her chest was bright red. She stood tall and particularly erect but wavered. She was in bad shape. She screamed, called us motherfuckers, pointed a manicured finger at each one of us. Eyeballed us. She was like, *alright, do you hear me, do you hear me.* We had better leave her son the fuck alone, goddamn Mexican motherfuckers. All mommie dearest.

What, like, no more wire hangers.

Yeah, it was crazy.

We were all quiet. We just looked at each other, trippin. Waiting for her to continue. Whoever was on Defender let it go and we heard the men in the game dying off. Periodic bursts. -boom, boom, boom- Ethan's mother walked to the train each morning. She wore slacks and two-inch heels to work. Most afternoons, she was at The Circle Club. Ethan took us with him when he went to see her. She sat in a red booth, her blouse loose and a tumbler in her hand like she just finished a set with Sammy Davis and Angie Dickinson. A single diamond pendant hung from her neck. Ethan blurted *Val* and she said *Hey babe. Tommy, get the boys some scallops. Good to see you, my handsome babe.* I didn't know what the fuck were scallops but I ate them. Ethan's mother ruffled her short hair as she chatted, a magnetic smirk when she listened to her companions, her arm lounging over the back of the booth. Smooches to her handsome babe. This time at the store she was different. It was dark and cold outside and she was in a skimpy dress like to go out dancing, the kind with little ass straps. Her eyes were tiny in her oversized glasses. Val stared us down, her arm motioning back and forth, marking us. Then she left. We stared at the doorway in case she came back. Someone said crazy bitch and we shifted to face the video game. Whoever had next dropped a quarter in the slot. Someone asked who in the group had been messing with Ethan so bad. Damn. Fuck if we knew. Whoever it was better leave Ethan the fuck alone before he got his ass beat. She was feeling to kill somebody. Someone about to get killt. Man, she called us goddamn Mexican motherfuckers. I ain't even Mexican. And I ain't no motherfucker. Fuckin Ruben's Filipino. Well, now he's fuckin Mexican. Trippin. See that, her titty was almost showing. The start button was slapped and the game overture rose. We huddled and squeezed in and went back to playing Defender.

Holy shit, dude. Fuck.
Yeah. Fuck.

It was true that we messed with her son, we messed with Ethan a lot, but everybody fucked with everybody. Bugged, talked shit. Some kids got picked on, but whatever. We were always fucking with each other. Always. All the time.

Ain't you fuckin Israel's brother? Yeah, you are. You look just like that punk ass.

The two dudes that passed through earlier were back. Neither one of us noticed them come in and we had no idea how long they had been there, standing against the rec center eating chips and smoking cigarettes. The dude talking, in the thick hood with the cholo devil, flicked his cigarette butt at us. Just like that punk ass, he said, drawing out the last sound, hissing.

Eusebio dropped off the bridge. I followed.

He stepped out and squared, fists at his sides.

What?

You must be a punk ass like your brother.

You don't know me, chump.

I know your brother. That's why you actin like you actin.

His partner howled, stamped a foot and smothered his hyena smile with his fist. He shook his friend like a rag doll. The dude in grey hood pulled his smokes out of his front pouch, and coolly lit a cigarette. He knew Eusebio wasn't about to do anything. He wasn't about shit. His partner howled again, disbelief at his friend's audacity. Straight called that fool out. Sucker. He was just like his brother. A little punk ass. Eusebio didn't say anything back. Dude in grey had the advantage. We didn't know what to expect. He could have a knife. He might be all talk. There wasn't anything to do at the moment but wait. Eusebio purposefully and slowly let spit dribble to the sand. Dude in grey blew smoke and harrumphed. He walked off and reached between some plants. He came back with a rock, passed it between hands like a juggler. We watched him keenly.

The dude in grey stopped, and dragged on his cigarette dramatic, his chin up, he was showing off. Then he passed the cigarette to his partner, put it directly into his mouth. The friend giggled girlish and turned away all self-conscious, *what are you doing*. He fluttered his hands against the cholo devil on dude's chest. Weird.

The dude in grey tossed the rock over his head from hand to hand. He smiled like a fool. Made wild mocking eyes. Then he feinted throwing the rock. We both flinched and they cracked up. Called us pussies. We kept watching. He feinted again, and then threw the rock by our heads. It wasn't close. It whizzed by. Then someone screamed. We turned around to find Rebecca with a can of Coke in each hand, crying, blood trailing from her hairline straight down her face. It dripped onto her white T-shirt. Annette called us motherfuckers. What did we fuckheads do. She gathered Rebecca's hair away from her face. Rebecca leaned forward to keep the blood off her clothes then got upset when it trickled over her shoes. She didn't bother to put the cans of Coke down.

There was a moment when we were all like whoa shit. Then Eusebio threw sand at the dude in grey's face like a move he had seen on TV and tackled him to the ground. He sat on his chest and punched hard and fast. He grabbed the fucker by the ears and began to knock his head against the pavement. Me and the other guy both jumped in. I didn't remember what or how, but we fought for a long time. Annette got in the fight. She clawed the dude in grey's face and then shuffled looking for an opening to kick him in the balls. I managed to get my arm under the friend's chin and closed him in a headlock. I tightened my grip and tried to choke the living shit out of him. He reached up and hooked a thumb in my eye. It hurt and scared me. I felt my eyeball pushed in. I leaned back and wrenched his neck. I yelled into his ear. Stupid motherfucker. There always had to be fuckheads like him, looking to mess with people. Annette kicked him and he moaned like he lost his breath. I didn't even know his stupid ass. Seb and me were just talking, kicking back. It was late and everybody was about to go home. Then these pricks showed up. The fucker pinched at my gut, used his fingernails. It hurt bad. I put my weight on the back of his neck. He flailed. The whole mass of bodies struggled. Annette kicked him again. He gurgled, fizzed. Nobody checked on Rebecca. She was still bleeding and crying. She sobbed, cussing. This dude shuddered and kicked violently with his heels in a last attempt to get loose. These motherfuckers. They needed to fuck with someone. All the time. Always.

Norman Antonio Zelaya was born and raised in San Francisco, CA. He has published stories in ZYZZYVA, NY Tyrant, 14 Hills, Cipactli, and Apogee Journal, among others. He was a 2015 Zoetrope: All-Story finalist, and a 2019 Anginas Scholarship recipient for latinx writers to attend the Community of Writers Workshops in Squaw Valley, CA. In 1997, he co-founded Los Delicados, and has performed extensively throughout the US with them. Zelaya has appeared on stage, in film and in the squared circle as luchador, Super Pulga. Orlando & Other Stories (Pochino Press, Oakland, Ca, 2017) was his first published book.

"There's a ship
The Black Freighter
With a skull on it's masthead
Will be coming in"

— Nina Simone, Pirate Jenny

Black Freighter Press publishes revolutionary books. committed to the exploration of liberation, using art to transform consciousness. A platform for Black and Brown writers to honor ancestry and propel radical imagination.

CPSIA information can be obtained
at www.ICGtesting.com
Printed in the USA
BVHW060403200722
642186BV00008B/33

9 781955 953009